Foreword

Foreword by the Secretary of State for Children, Schools and Families and the Secretary of State for Culture, Media and Sport

Fun and exciting opportunities to play are at the heart of a happy, healthy and enjoyable childhood. Better outdoor play opportunities are good for children, good for families and good for communities.

Time and space to play safely is integral to our ambition to make England the best country in the world for children and young people to grow up – it is vital to children's physical, emotional, social and educational development.

Our vision, backed by an investment of £235 million, is to make sure that every residential area has a variety of high-quality places for all children to play safely and free of charge. This is a direct response to demands from children, young people and their families for better play facilities in every area.

In April, our *Fair Play* consultation set out an ambitious range of proposals to make a reality of our vision for world-class play opportunities. This consultation attracted an overwhelming response, with 9,400 children and young people letting us know how they would like the Government to support their play. Twelve percent of these responses came from disabled children, reinforcing the need to do even more to make sure that we make play accessible for all children, regardless of their circumstances.

The enthusiastic support for our proposals in *Fair Play* underpins this first national Play Strategy for England. The Strategy sets out in more detail how we will deliver our capital investment programme from 2008 to 2011 so that up to 3,500 new and refurbished play sites reflect the needs of children, parents and the local community in every area. The accelerated roll-out of our new investment means that every local authority will have been offered at least £1million of capital funding by April 2009, so that better facilities can be made available to children sooner.

We are delighted to see the first new outdoor play areas being built across the country – and to hear how much these improvements are valued by local communities.

As a result of our investment and the implementation of this Play Strategy, led locally by Children's Trusts, we want at least 100,000 more children to tell us every year that their local play areas and parks are good or very good. Increasing levels of satisfaction in local authorities will show us that we are successful in developing more child-friendly communities, which value children's play and provide better environments for children and young people to enjoy.

We know that we can only achieve our vision for play in 2020 by working in partnership with local and national delivery partners, including the third sector, and by putting children, young people and their parents at the heart of the design and development of neighbourhood provision.

We hope to build on the huge interest and engagement with our consultation earlier this year to deliver the improvement in local play facilities that every family wants.

Rt Hon Ed Balls MP
Secretary of State for Children, Schools and Families

Rt Hon Andy Burnham MP
Secretary of State for Culture, Media and Sport

Children playing at the opening of a Playbuilder site in Denstone, Staffordshire

Executive summary

Introduction

1. The Government's ambition is to make this the best country in the world for children to grow up. Children, young people and their parents all recognise that play is a vital ingredient of a happy and healthy childhood, supporting children's physical, emotional, social and educational development.

2. This national Play Strategy, backed by £235 million of dedicated investment for local play facilities across the country, is informed by extensive consultation with children, young people and their parents.

3. Our *Fair Play* consultation, launched in April 2008, attracted a huge response. Over 9,400 children and young people shared their views with us, giving widespread support for our 2020 vision for play in every residential area.

4. Our aim, shared with children, young people and parents, is for all children to be able to enjoy a range of safe and exciting places to play close to where they live. Through children and communities' involvement in the design and planning of these spaces, play areas will be valued locally and continue to reflect the distinct needs of each community.

5. This Strategy sets out how we will deliver our vision for 2020, supporting local delivery partners to make a reality of children's right to play, as stated in Article 31 of the United Nations Convention on the Rights of the Child.

Our vision for play

- In every residential area there are a variety of supervised and unsupervised places for play, free of charge;

- Local neighbourhoods are, and feel like, safe, interesting places to play;

- Routes to children's play space are safe and accessible for all children and young people;

- Parks and open spaces are attractive and welcoming to children and young people, and are well maintained and well used;

- Children and young people have a clear stake in public space and their play is accepted by their neighbours;

- Children and young people play in a way that respects other people and property;

- Children and young people and their families take an active role in the development of local play spaces; and

- Play spaces are attractive, welcoming, engaging and accessible for all local children and young people, including disabled children, and children from minority groups in the community.

Delivering our vision for play

6. Chapter 2, 'Our vision for 2020', sets out the short, medium and long-term objectives that will deliver our vision for play.

Short term: 2008–2011

7. Through the development and implementation of this national Strategy, backed by dedicated investment, our immediate priority is to increase the availability of safe, exciting and inclusive play facilities, putting the needs of local communities at the heart of the design process and improving facilities in the areas where children need them most. We will establish a strong framework for local delivery, including continuing to develop the compelling evidence base on the benefits of play and identifying and disseminating best practice to help our partners deliver high-quality local play spaces.

Medium term: 2011–2014

8. Over the medium term, we will build on our initial investment and support Children's Trusts to provide the local leadership necessary to build communities that value and respond to children, young people and parents' demands for safe and well-maintained places to play. This will rely on staff from across wider local authority and health services understanding and supporting this agenda, integrating it within local children's services. Progress will be demonstrated year-on-year by higher reported satisfaction of children with local outdoor play facilities. Those who support and supervise children's play will become increasingly professionalised, ensuring staffed provision is high quality and makes the right links with other children's services locally.

Long term: 2014–2020

9. Over the longer term, our objective is that all children and young people will be able to access world-class play and recreation spaces near where they live, within communities that are child-friendly. Children's Trusts will lead the delivery of excellent local play provision, with consideration of children's needs embedded in the planning of the wider Local Strategic Partnership.

10. This rest of this Strategy sets out in detail how we will work with local partners to deliver this vision across the country.

Chapter 3: More places to play

11. Children and parents told us that they want more high-quality places to play near where they live. To respond to this demand, our aim is to provide a variety of safe, accessible and exciting places to play in every residential area.

Children, young people and adults asked for:

- More play spaces, accessible to all children throughout the country;

- Play spaces that are exciting and stimulating for children, especially 8–13 year olds;

- Play spaces where families can share and enjoy leisure time; and

- Places to play when the weather is bad.

Our key actions:

- We are investing £235 million in up to 3,500 play areas across the country;

- We are investing in 30 Pathfinder local authorities to receive additional funding, part of which will be used to develop a large, staffed adventure playground;

- Every local authority will receive at least £1 million in funding, to be targeted on the children most in need of improved play opportunities;

- So that children can benefit from this investment as soon as possible, we are accelerating national roll-out so that every local authority will be offered funding by April 2009;

- We have contracted Play England as our national delivery partner and significantly expanded their capacity. Play England will provide all local authorities with access to expertise, planning advice and guidance;

- We have published detailed design guidance to help local partners produce the new and refurbished play areas that children and parents tell us they want to see; and

- We will explore how good play opportunities can be provided when the weather makes outdoor play unappealing to children.

Chapter 4: Supporting play throughout childhood

12. Children of all ages want to have opportunities to play, regardless of their background, physical ability and where they live. To improve opportunities for all children, the Strategy focuses on places where children and young people spend their leisure time (including parks and green spaces), schools and Sure Start Children's Centres. Through the implementation of this Strategy, we will make sure that parents know what opportunities exist locally.

Children, young people and adults asked for:

- Improved play opportunities for all children in schools, children's centres and through other local services;

- Improved provision and access for children least able to take advantage of play opportunities;

- Play spaces that are exciting and accessible for children with disabilities; and

- Better information about what is available locally.

Our key actions:

- By April 2009, we will publish a toolkit to help local authorities and service providers inform parents and children about local play opportunities;

- To ensure disabled children benefit fully from our investment in play we have introduced funding requirements and are working with the third sector to provide expertise, advice and guidance for local authorities;

- New Sure Start Children's Centres will deliver best practice in design and provision of spaces for children to play; and

- The Building Schools for the Future capital investment programme will have clear requirements around outdoor play and recreational spaces in schools.

Chapter 5: Playing safely

13. Children, young people and parents told us that concerns about safety are preventing children from going outside and accessing play areas, and that play facilities are often dull and are not challenging and stimulating for children. To address this, we will do more to tackle bullying and crime, improve road safety and increase the availability of appropriately supervised play, as well as to support partners to deliver safe and exciting play areas that children and young people want to see.

Children, young people and adults asked for:

- Steps to address fears of bullying and crime;

- Increased supervision of play spaces, but without turning play into a regimented, structured activity;

- Safer routes to play spaces;

- Play spaces that are clean and well maintained;

- Play spaces that are exciting and help children learn how to take and manage risks in a safe environment; and

- Those working in local areas asked for support on the issue of litigation around play-related accidents.

Our key actions:

- We will publish guidance for practitioners on tackling bullying outside schools;

- We are taking steps to tackle youth-related crime through the *Youth Crime Action Plan* and the *Youth Taskforce Action Plan*;

- We are supporting links between local authorities, the third sector and community policing to improve appropriate supervision of children playing;

- Alongside this Strategy, we are launching pilot schemes to develop models for local volunteering to supervise children playing; and

- We are publishing guidance on proportionate risk management to support the delivery of exciting play spaces.

Chapter 6: Child-friendly communities

14. We want to see communities that give greater consideration to children's needs and interests – communities which are more

child-friendly. Children and young people want their own views to be reflected in local decisions about how their neighbourhoods are designed and developed. In response to this, we are taking steps to make local areas more child-friendly and more welcoming for children, in particular, by working with local partners and the housing industry.

Children, young people and adults asked for:

- Children, young people and local communities to be involved throughout the design and construction of play spaces;

- Children to be able to play in public space, streets and neighbourhoods; and

- Communities to become more tolerant and welcoming of children's play as long as children respect the views of others.

Our key actions:

- We will ensure that children's needs are fully reflected in a forthcoming review of planning policy;

- New web-based guidance will bring together best practice for planning officers on supporting children's play and recreation;

- A new national partnership will deliver training to every local authority by March 2011, focused on helping the professionals who design and manage our neighbourhoods to understand the importance of play and child-friendly spaces;

- We are working with the social housing sector and regulators to ensure that play is supported in some of the most deprived areas;

- The Commission for Architecture and the Built Environment is working with the Government, local authorities, and the housing development industry to deliver residential developments and new housing growth areas that meet children's needs and interests; and

- Our *Aiming High* strategy is taking steps to foster a more positive approach to young people across society.

Chapter 7: Embedding play in local priorities

15. Parents want play to continue to be a priority for the Government and local authorities and we also want to ensure that our investment will have a lasting impact. To achieve this we will create a policy framework and incentives for sustainable and effective delivery in every area and invest in a skilled workforce. This will be driven by a shared understanding across local partners and local communities on the value of play, what good play opportunities look like and where they are needed, and what the various roles and responsibilities should be locally to deliver on this.

National and local delivery partners asked for:

- Action to ensure play becomes a priority, with respondents welcoming the national indicator;

- Play to have a higher priority locally and be embedded in children's services and wider local authority business planning;

- The health sector to play a key role in supporting and promoting play;

- Support for the playwork profession and recognition of their commitment; and

- The third sector to receive support, as a crucial delivery partner.

Our key actions:

- We are introducing a new national indicator from April 2009 for local authorities, which will ask children how satisfied they are with their local parks and play areas;

- Updated statutory guidance for Children's Trusts sets out roles and responsibilities in relation to play;

- Jointly with Play England, we are publishing for consultation new draft guidance on how Children's Trusts and Local Strategic Partnerships can respond to children's play needs as they plan services and changes to neighbourhoods;

- We are working with the Department of Health to support active play as part of the drive by Children's Trusts to help children lead healthy lives, and through the healthy lifestyle campaign Play4Life;

- We are enabling 4,000 playworkers to achieve a level 3 playwork qualification by 2011;

- We are supporting the continuous professional development of leaders and managers in the play workforce by developing a new playwork management qualification; and

- We are investing £1.5 million in third sector-run adventure playgrounds and providing funding to help build third sector infrastructure that will support play locally.

16. This Strategy aims to make a reality of our ambition for world-class opportunities for play in every area, by helping professionals in local government, the third sector and business to respond to the play and recreational needs of children and young people.

Photo: Play England

Chapter 1
Our vision for 2020

1.1 The Play Strategy is key to achieving our ambition to make this the best place in the world for children and young people to grow up. Play is a vital ingredient of a happy and healthy childhood.

Defining play

This Strategy defines play as children and young people following their own ideas and interests, in their own way and for their own reasons, having fun while respecting themselves and others

---

1.2 This Strategy strongly reflects the core principles of *The Children's Plan*[1] that:

- children and young people should be able to enjoy their childhood, as well as grow up prepared for adult life;

- the Government should do more to back parents and families in bringing up children; and

- services should be shaped by and responsive to children, young people and families rather than designed around professionals.

1.3 Through the implementation of this Strategy, we will respond to the demands of children, young people and their parents for more high-quality, safe and exciting places to play in their neighbourhood. This will make a reality of children's right to play, as stated in Article 31 of the UN Convention on the Rights of the Child.

Our vision for play

1.4 In response to the *Fair Play* consultation, published in April 2008, children, young people, parents, local services, expert stakeholders and the wider public offered widespread support for our vision for play:

- in every residential area there are a variety of supervised and unsupervised places for play, free of charge;

- local neighbourhoods are, and feel like, safe, interesting places to play;

- routes to children's play space are safe and accessible for all children and young people;

- parks and open spaces are attractive and welcoming to children and young people, and are well maintained and well used;

- children and young people have a clear stake in public space and their play is accepted by their neighbours;

- children and young people play in a way that respects other people and property;

- children and young people and their families take an active role in the development of local play spaces; and

- play spaces are attractive, welcoming, engaging and accessible for all local children and young people, including disabled children, and children from minority groups in the community.

1.5 To achieve this vision, the *Fair Play* document outlined the Government's proposals to:

- invest £235 million over 2008–11 to develop up to 3,500 public play areas;

- support 30 local authorities to develop adventure playgrounds or play parks aimed at 8-13 year olds in disadvantaged areas (20 were announced in April and a further 10 have been announced alongside this publication);

- work with councils to ensure play areas are stimulating, exciting and attractive to children – ensuring the involvement of children, families and communities;

- drive local performance with a new national indicator from 2009;

Children in Leicester consider plans with an architect as part of the area's Playbuilder programme

- develop and test volunteering opportunities to support play;

- work with planners, developers and transport officers to create neighbourhoods that meet the needs of children and families; and

- boost the qualifications and skills of the workforce that supports and supervises play.

1.6   There was a huge response to *Fair Play*. Over 9,400 children responded to the consultation, of which 72% said that our plans would make a positive difference to them. In addition, 84% of adults thought that the Government had set out the right vision and set of aims for play in England. A summary of our evidence base on the benefits of play and the problems children and young people face is available at www.dcsf.gov.uk/play

1.7   This publication outlines our short, medium and long-term objectives to deliver the Play Strategy vision.

Short term: 2008–2011

1.8   Through the development and implementation of this national Strategy, backed by dedicated investment, our immediate priority is to increase the availability of safe, exciting and inclusive play facilities, putting the needs of local communities at the heart of the design process and improving facilities in the areas where children need them most. We will establish a strong framework and clear roles and responsibilities for local delivery. We will also continue to develop the compelling evidence base on the benefits of play and identify and disseminate best practice to help our partners deliver high-quality local play spaces.

Medium term: 2011–2014

1.9   Over the medium term, we will work to build on our initial investment and support Children's Trusts to provide the local leadership necessary to build communities that value and respond to children, young people and parents' demands for safe, exciting and well-maintained places to play. Staff from across wider local authority and health services will understand and support this agenda. Progress will be demonstrated year-on-year by higher reported satisfaction of children with local outdoor play facilities. Play spaces and routes to play will be safer and parents will believe this to be the case. An increasingly professionalised play workforce will ensure staffed provision is of high quality, and embedded within integrated children's services locally.

Long term: 2014–2020

1.10 Over the longer term, our objective is that all children and young people will be able to access world-class play and recreation spaces near where they live within communities that are more child-friendly. Children's Trusts will lead the delivery of excellent local play provision, with consideration of children's needs embedded in the planning of the wider Local Strategic Partnership.

1.11 This will mean that our built environment is designed and managed in a way that supports play. It will mean that children, young people and parents will be at the heart of decisions about local play provision, and communities will accept and support children playing in public. And because neighbourhoods will be safer, with more adults looking out for children, parents will feel more confident about choosing to let their children play outside alone or with their friends.

Our actions to deliver

1.12 As set out in this Strategy, we are already making progress in neighbourhoods across the country to deliver these objectives. However, we need to do more to ensure that all children are able to enjoy opportunities for play in their local area.

Photo: Play England

1.13 This Strategy sets out five overarching areas of action to improve play opportunities for all children:

- **More places to play:** responding to children's demands for high-quality play spaces in every area;

- **Supporting play throughout childhood:** improving provision through a range of settings for children of all ages;

- **Playing safely:** providing safe, accessible and stimulating places for children to play;

- **Child-friendly communities:** engaging communities and involving children in decisions; and

- **Embedding play in local priorities:** ensuring leadership and effective delivery in every local area.

1.14 Chapters 3–7 outline the feedback and proposals we received through the *Fair Play* consultation on each of these areas and set out our actions to address the needs of children, young people and families.

Chapter 2
The Fair Play consultation

2.1 The Government's *Fair Play* consultation was launched in April 2008, setting out the Government's vision and proposals on play, structured around the priorities identified by research and through consultation with parents, play experts, and children.

2.2 The vision and proposals set out in Fair Play were strongly supported by professionals working in the play sector, local delivery partners, the wider public and through a separate consultation designed for children and young people.

- In the adults' consultation, 84% of respondents thought that the Government had set out the right national vision and set of aims for play in England.

- In the children's consultation, 72% of children thought that our plan to make more and safer areas for them to play in would make a positive difference to them.

2.3 The following paragraphs summarise the key messages that emerged from the consultation.

What children told us...

2.4 We wanted to hear from as many children as possible, and therefore designed different consultation materials tailored for adults and children. The children's version was launched alongside the adult materials, and was very successful in reaching children. Overall, 9,409 children responded, 12% of whom were children with disabilities. Children's favourite option was to reply through an online game, which let them build their own virtual play area. By answering the questions, respondents could gain credits which then let them choose slides, swings, climbing walls and other equipment to add to their ideal play space.

2.5 Most children (72%) agreed that our proposals would help to provide more and safer areas for them to play and felt that this would make them and their parents/carers feel happier about them playing outside more often.

Communities supporting play

2.6 Children thought that a range of people could help children have more fun outside their home. Children thought that the local community could be more tolerant, parents and carers could get more involved in their play, the Government could invest more money and schools could provide more opportunities for play.

Barriers to outdoor play

2.7   A lack of places to go and things to do was the main reason children said they did not play outside, followed by concern for their own safety, the cost of play activities and a preference to stay at home. Other reasons included bad weather, their parents' and carers' reluctance to allow them out to play, difficulties in travelling to play areas and a lack of people to go with.

2.8   The greatest barrier identified by 8–13 year olds was a lack of safe and clean play areas near to their homes. They wanted to have more interesting things to do such as better play equipment and activities, places to meet friends and school grounds to use outside school hours.

2.9   Designating specific areas in which children can play in was considered to be the best way to prevent them being stopped from playing for no reason. Children also thought that it would help if their neighbours were more tolerant and if playworkers, particularly those closer to their own age, were present.

Supporting children with disabilities

2.10   Overall, children considered that those with disabilities should have the same access to play opportunities as their peers. They felt that children with disabilities would be

Children considering plans for a new play site in Leicester, as part of the area's Playbuilder programme

better able to play alongside others if they had people to help them and by improving access to play areas that are adapted for their use.

Involving children in designing play areas

2.11 Most children were keen to be involved in creating new play areas by choosing the apparatus and facilities, helping to build them and deciding on the best location. Respondents believed that involving children would help to engender a sense of ownership which would ensure that play areas were well kept and well used.

2.12 Children had many ideas for making it easier and more fun to play outside. Their main priorities were to make more, bigger, better, safer and cleaner play areas with more exciting, varied and challenging equipment and activities. They also wanted to see separate play areas for younger and older children and more play areas that disabled children could use.

Playing safely

2.13 Safety was a key factor affecting children's enjoyment of their playtime, with most wanting safer play areas and roads. Many expressed concerns about intimidation by older children and suggested that having more adults around, such as playworkers, wardens and police patrols, would make them feel less at risk from harm.

Informing children and parents about play

2.14 Children believed that a range of methods should be used to let them and their parents/carers know about good places to play, including signs saying 'children play here', information in schools, leaflets, adverts in the local media and on television, using the internet and mailshots.

What adults told us...

2.15 The adult version of the consultation attracted 234 responses. The highest numbers of responses came from local authorities (65), charities (38), national/commercial organisations (29), play organisations (29), parents (20) and professionals working with children (18).

2.16 Overall respondents welcomed the proposals (84%) and agreed with the visions and aims for play in England. Respondents agreed that the introduction of a play indicator for local areas, highlighting children's views on local play provision, was a good idea. Respondents were content that the areas identified for action were correct and suggested that sufficient funding and raising the profile of play in the community were important issues.

Communities supporting play

2.17 Most respondents felt that parents were responsible for helping children to play but suggested that others such as local authorities, schools and communities all have an important role. Respondents believed that schools could open their grounds up after school hours and during school holidays to increase the opportunities children have to play.

The need to improve facilities

2.18 Respondents said that the biggest gap in play providing generally was simply a lack of suitable play areas in their communities and the poor condition of some existing facilities. Respondents wanted improved surfaces for wheelchair users, more parking areas near to sites and toilet facilities. Access to play areas was seen as one area that could be improved to allow disabled children to take advantage of the same opportunities.

Playing safely

2.19   Respondents said that safety was a big issue that stopped children from playing, both on routes to play areas and at play areas themselves. Respondents suggested lower speed limits and improved road safety measures as ways to combat this. Respondents wanted more exciting play areas for children and young people with more challenging equipment and thought that involving children in the design process would help them feel ownership and make them more likely to look after play areas.

2.20   Respondents felt that more supervision of play areas would be beneficial as parents may allow their children out to play more if they felt they were being supervised. However, respondents expressed a concern that play should not be turned into an overly regimented activity. Instead, it was felt that play needs to be spontaneous and child-led, and adult supervision needs to respect and enable this. Respondents also wanted children to be able to travel safely and enjoy clean, well-looked-after play areas and action to address bullying and anti-social behaviour. Respondents also believed that more positive stories about children and young people's achievements in the media would help reassure parents' concerns about allowing children to play outside.

2.21   Respondents said that how, when and by whom children needed to be supervised depended on the age of the children and the context in which they were playing. Respondents also recognised the value of unsupervised play.

Involving communities

2.22   Respondents felt that it was important that communities became more tolerant of children playing in and around the streets in their neighbourhood. They also said that parents volunteering in the community and taking time to play outside with their children had positive benefits for all.

Other issues

2.23   Respondents believed that the fear of being sued had led to play areas becoming less interesting to children and that designing equipment to lessen injury from accidents was now the norm. Respondents believed that Primary Care Trusts had a vital role to play advertising the benefits of play in relation to children and young people's physical and mental health. Respondents also felt that playworkers were key to the success of the Government's Play Strategy.

2.24   As set out in each of the following chapters, the Play Strategy directly responds to the views articulated in the *Fair Play* consultation.

Chapter 3
More places to play

One of the strongest messages we received through our *Fair Play* consultation was that children and parents want more places to play near where they live. This Strategy responds to children's demands to be able to find places near their homes where they can play freely and meet their friends. The delivery of this Strategy will mean that every residential area will have a variety of safe, accessible and exciting places to play.

The Government is investing significantly in new and improved play spaces that can be used free of charge by all children, with a particular focus on 8–13 year olds. These play spaces are being developed by top tier local authorities in partnership with children, young people, families, communities, the third sector and district, parish and town councils. In 63 local authorities across the country work is already well underway, with sites already open and the number of play spaces increasing every month.

Key actions:

- We are investing £235 million in up to 3,500 play areas across the country;

- We are investing in 30 Pathfinder local authorities to receive additional funding, part of which will be used to develop a large, staffed adventure playground;

- Every local authority will receive at least £1 million in funding, to be targeted on the children most in need of improved play opportunities;

- So that children can benefit from this investment as soon as possible, we are accelerating roll-out so that every local authority will be offered funding by April 2009;

- We have contracted Play England as our national delivery partner and significantly expanded their capacity. Play England will provide all local authorities with access to expertise, planning advice and guidance;

- We have published detailed design guidance to help local partners produce the new and refurbished play areas that children and parents tell us they want to see; and

- We will explore how good play opportunities can be provided when the weather makes outdoor play unappealing to children.

The consultation response

Children and young people told us…

When asked what stops them spending time outdoors, 54% of children responding said it was because they had nowhere to go and nothing to do. Reasons given included:

- that there were no play areas near where they lived;

- that existing play areas were boring or unsuitable for their age group, particularly for older children; and

- the cost of activities and transport to good quality play spaces prevented many children from spending time outdoors.

A number of children also commented that bad weather, parents' attitudes, the location of play areas, disabilities, homework and having no one to play with prevented them from playing outdoors.

Adults told us…

When asked what parents and children see as the biggest gap in the play facilities that are currently available to them, 63% of respondents simply said that there was a general lack of facilities.

Respondents called for an increased number of good quality and easily accessible play spaces, stimulating play equipment, more play provision targeted at under 8s and children aged 13 to 18, facilities to be kept in a good condition, family-friendly spaces and for play areas to be free of charge.

Investing in public play spaces

We are investing £235 million in up to 3,500 play areas across the country

3.1   We are investing ring-fenced funding to deliver safe, accessible and exciting play areas in every local area. Our delivery partner, Play England, is supporting local authorities with their project planning and work to ensure that these play areas are well designed, meet local children's needs and are accessible to children of all abilities and backgrounds.

We are investing in 30 Pathfinder local authorities to receive additional funding, part of which will be used to develop a large, staffed adventure playground

3.2   Every local authority will be designated as either a Pathfinder or Playbuilder.

Play Pathfinders:

Thirty local authorities will be Play Pathfinders. The first wave of 20 Play Pathfinders will receive approximately £2 million of capital funding over 2008–10 and £500,000 revenue funding over 2008–11.

The second wave, 10 further Pathfinders, will receive the same allocation but over 2009–11.

Each Pathfinder authority will develop at least 28 public play spaces in their local area, as well as at least one adventure playground. They will also test a variety of innovative approaches to supporting and creating play spaces for their local communities.

Playbuilders:

All other local authorities will be designated Playbuilders and will each receive approximately £1.1 million capital investment[1] to develop at least 22 public play spaces in their local area.

Local authorities told us they needed help to support projects, and we will also therefore make a revenue payment of around £45,000 in total to every Playbuilder authority as a contribution towards their initial set-up costs.

The Conditions of funding for Pathfinders and Playbuilders require them to set out satisfactorily in project plans how they will:

- provide innovative and stimulating equipment and landscaping on sites;

- involve children and young people, parents, carers and the wider community and locally-elected members in the decisions about where and how funding will be spent;

- ensure better access and experiences for disabled children;

- ensure that children are able to travel to and from play areas in safety; and

- ensure that the capital investment is sustainable in terms of protection of sites against vandalism, and ongoing maintenance.

Focusing investment on deprived areas

Every local authority will receive at least £1 million in funding, to be targeted on the children most in need of improved play opportunities

3.3   We are ensuring that our new funding helps those children and families that need it most. All authorities across the programme will be required to show in their project plans how they will target investment on local children most in need of better facilities, and in selecting our Pathfinders, we have given specific consideration to how authorities demonstrated a focus on deprived areas. Our funding allocations to all authorities are weighted by their relative deprivation level. On the ground, we are already seeing improvements in some of the poorest areas, including through joint projects between local authorities and Registered Social Landlords.

The next stage of the capital programme

So that children can benefit from this investment as soon as possible, we are accelerating roll-out so that every local authority will be offered funding by April 2009

3.4   In April 2008, we announced the first 20 Pathfinder local authorities, and the first 43 Playbuilder local authorities. Alongside the launch of this publication, we have now announced:

- The 10 final Pathfinder authorities who will commence work in April 2009; and

- An offer of Playbuilder funding from April 2009 for the remaining 86 local authorities who are not already part of the programme.

3.5   A full list of announced Pathfinder authorities is provided at Annex A, and a full list of Playbuilder authorities is provided at www.dcsf.gov.uk/play

---

1   Bespoke allocations for Rutland, Isles of Scilly and the City of London will be agreed with these authorities.

3.6   We have brought forward our investment programme to enable children across the country to benefit sooner from improved play spaces. Bringing forward the investment will also give the local authorities who would otherwise have been coming later into our programme more time to plan and consult.

3.7   We will work closely with the building and landscaping industries, and with the manufacturers of play equipment through bodies such as the Association of Play Industries, to ensure that there is good planning around the services and equipment that local authorities will need and adequate capacity from suppliers to meet demand.

Case study: Play Pathfinder progress in Dudley

In April 2008, Dudley Children's Services was awarded Play Pathfinder status and will be improving 28 children's play areas across the borough, as well as building a new adventure playground. The authority consulted with children, young people and the local community, and this highlighted the needs of children with disabilities and learning difficulties as a key priority.

To meet this priority, Dudley are using part of the Pathfinder funding to create a new, purpose-built adventure playground for children between the ages of 8 to 13, which will provide excellent play facilities for children with disabilities. A new children's play service is also being established with third sector providers KIDS and me2Mencap.

Since April, new activities and play facilities have been provided in public parks, including specialised equipment for those children who use a wheelchair. Young people with a disability have also taken on the role of volunteer play rangers to help other disabled children to play outside safely.

Children in Dudley discuss plans to transform a local play site, as part of the area's Pathfinder programme

Case study: Playbuilder progress in Thurrock

Thurrock was designated as a Playbuilder authority in April 2008 and progress is well underway to transform play spaces for children in the area.

Fobbing Recreational Ground was one of the areas selected for investment, as local children in Fobbing were in particular need of a high-quality place to play. Local children were asked to illustrate and talk about their favourite play activities and design their spaces. They looked at the *Design for Play* guidance, which encouraged great discussion, and their ideas were built into the final design. They were concerned about safe access to the park and their ideas have been taken to the local highways authority to come up with a solution.

The site opened in time for half term and the children and their families planted 25 trees – one for each Playbuilder site – and a daffodil maze to mark the occasion. Parents have now offered to monitor the site, and are searching for other funding for a toddler's play space and to help develop more natural play opportunities and landscaping.

Expert support for local authorities

We have contracted Play England as our national delivery partner and significantly expanded their capacity. Play England will provide all local authorities with access to expertise, planning advice and guidance

3.8   To support authorities in making best use of the funding available, DCSF have appointed Play England as their national delivery partner to work closely with the Government Offices to ensure effective project planning and provide packages of support and challenge to every local authority, promote good practice in local delivery and strategic planning, and build the capacity of the voluntary and community sector.

3.9   Play England is part of the National Children's Bureau. Through its nine regional offices, the organisation will support the Play Pathfinders and Playbuilders with:

- resources and information on designing play spaces;

- support with strategic planning and delivery;

- training, conferences and seminars;

- networking and referrals to other professional sources of support; and

- advocacy and campaigning support.

3.10   National and regional good practice sharing networks have been established to ensure that lessons learned are captured and shared with other authorities.

3.11   More information and contact details for each Play England regional team can be found at www.playengland.org.uk

Additional Play England regional workers

3.12   Local authorities already involved in the programme have told us that they are benefiting from Play England's support and that more help would be welcome. As the number of Pathfinder and Playbuilder local authorities grows from April 2009, we want to ensure that all local authorities have access to

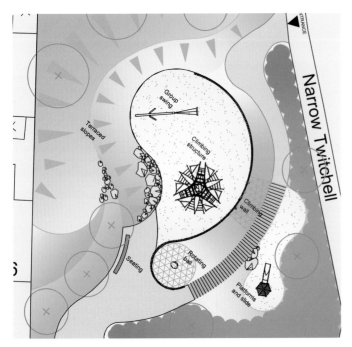

Plans for a new play area in Rotherham, as part of the area's Pathfinder programme

excellent support to ensure they can deliver on their projects. We are therefore funding additional Play England workers, and there will be one full-time development officer dedicated to our programme in every Government Office region.

Involving children, families and communities

3.13 We know that communities feel a greater sense of ownership and pride where they have been involved in creating a play area from the outset.

3.14 We have therefore required local authorities to ensure that children, parents and local communities are involved throughout the capital programme and that the play spaces are designed and delivered to meet local needs and reflect local input. Supporting and funding community-led projects is a specific condition of our grants to local authorities.

3.15 To support this, we are providing funding for Play England, to work with established community support organisations and put local authorities in touch with a team of professionals who will provide over 2,500 hours of consultancy across the programme to support the development of community-led projects and help increase the role of the third sector.

3.16 In addition, we have asked Play England to revise and update the *Neighbourhood Play Toolkit*.[2] Play England has appointed Play Association Tower Hamlets (PATH) to undertake a review and revision of the toolkit and a revised version will be available in summer 2009. Created in consultation with local neighbourhood play projects, this resource shows how to support community-led projects on play.

Creating exciting play spaces

We have published detailed design guidance to help local partners produce the new and refurbished play areas that children and parents tell us they want to see

3.17 Children told us through the consultation that they wanted more stimulating and exciting places to play. In August 2008, we jointly published with Play England a guidance document called *Design for Play: A guide to creating successful play spaces*. We have already issued over 10,000 print copies and, in addition, over 14,000 copies have been downloaded.

2   Topics include: making groups work; involving young children and the community; audit, funding and insurance; design; health and safety; and working with the media.

> ## Case study: ensuring child-friendly play design in Bath and North East Somerset
>
> Bath and North East Somerset was designated as a Play Pathfinder in April 2008. In total, 28 play sites will be developed and renovated in the local area, alongside the development of a large adventure play park and skatepark. The authority have taken significant steps to ensure that design and planning processes take into account the needs and interests of children.
>
> To recognise the fact that playworkers are vital to making sure that local issues for children and young people are heard and translated into designs, each play provider is linked to a play space designer. The authority has also drawn on the *Design For Play* guidance and expertise from Play England in drawing up plans for its new play sites.
>
> The voluntary sector, play rangers, playworkers, and local parents have all helped involve communities in the design of the new play spaces, including children and young people.

3.18 *Design for Play* supports good practice in the development and improvement of public play space. It provides guiding principles that will support local authorities in allocating the capital funding we are investing in play spaces. The guide shows how to design excellent play spaces, which can be affordably maintained, which give children and young people the freedom to play creatively, and yet still allow them to experience risk, challenge and excitement. It is available free of charge, either as a print publication or to download from www.playengland.org.uk

3.19 Alongside this Strategy, we are publishing *Managing Risk in Play Provision Implementation Guide*. This guide shows play providers how to develop proportionate risk assessment practices that take account of the benefits to children and young people of exciting and challenging play experiences. Further details on this guide are provided in Chapter 5, 'Playing safely'.

Sites where families can enjoy time together

3.20 The consultation responses included a strong call for sites that can cater for a range of ages and which offer amenities for adults. This has been reflected in the *Design for Play* guide, and will help local authorities consider these issues as they roll-out their capital projects locally.

Maintenance of play facilities

3.21 We know that children, young people and their parents want play sites to be well maintained. This is why we will use approximately £5.5 million to provide every Playbuilder authority with an average payment of £45,000 to help cover initial set-up costs for projects and to support them in developing local infrastructure to sustain maintenance over the longer term.

3.22 The *Design for Play* guide from Play England shows authorities how to invest in durable equipment and use natural materials and settings that cost less to maintain. The Strategy's emphasis on community engagement and increasing supervision should also reduce the costs of vandalism.

We have outlined actions in Chapter 6, 'Embedding play in local priorities', to encourage play as a priority for Children's Trusts, and we have already seen Pathfinder and Playbuilder authorities integrating play within wider local service provision and long-established play area maintenance programmes, in order to ensure improved play spaces.

Work begins at a new play site in Wolverhampton, as part of their Pathfinder programme

Good quality indoor play provision

We will explore how good play opportunities can be provided when the weather makes outdoor play unappealing to children

3.23   Children told us through the consultation that they have fewer opportunities to play when the weather is bad. We have listened to these concerns and will work with our Pathfinders and with stakeholders to explore any opportunities relating to indoor play provision. All the new Pathfinder adventure playgrounds will have warm, well-equipped indoor play areas, and there may also be some scope for local delivery partners to consider subsidised indoor provision, sponsorship arrangements or other solutions to meet children's demand for indoor play opportunities. A key principle of the Play Strategy is that play opportunities must be affordable and accessible to all children, and this principle will be integral to this

A completed Playbuilder site in Taunton Deane, Somerset. Photo provided by Proludic

exploratory work around indoor play facilities.

The progress so far

3.24 The 63 top tier local authorities designated as the first wave of Pathfinder and Playbuilder authorities are now undertaking a process of consulting their local communities, planning, designing and building new or refurbished play spaces for their local areas.

3.25 By the end of March 2009, there will be over 500 play spaces being built for children, young people and communities to enjoy. These include play spaces in rural and urban areas. We have been clear that the play spaces must meet local needs and will be located to meet this need.

Early evaluation findings

3.26 We commissioned Ipsos MORI to carry out some early qualitative research with parents and children, ahead of our main evaluation fieldwork, to help understand their experiences of recently improved play areas.[3] Both children and parents tended to be overwhelmingly positive about the improvements and felt they had benefited from them and the new approach to design. They suggested that the improvements tended to increase their enjoyment of play areas and encourage them to stay longer for each visit.

3.27 Both children and parents tended to be positive about supervised play areas, some children associating these with a sense of freedom, away from their parents' watch.

2   In-depth interviews with parents and children were carried out in October and November 2008 based on experiences of seven play areas across England that had recently been improved by BIG Lottery or Sure Start funding. The improvements at these sites were based around 10 good practice principles of designing successful play spaces. It is these 10 principles that are contained within our *Design for Play* guidance document and which we encourage play Pathfinders and Playbuilders to take account of when planning how to make best use of their capital funding. As the research is qualitative and based on a small number of interviews, findings provide useful insights but are not representative of all users or all newly-improved play areas. Findings here are based on a preliminary analysis of results; we will publish a full report in due course.

Chapter 4
Supporting play throughout childhood

Children of all ages want to have opportunities to play, regardless of their background, physical ability and where they live. To improve opportunities for all children, the Strategy focuses on places where children and young people spend their leisure time (including parks and green spaces), schools and Sure Start Children's Centres. Through the implementation of this Strategy, we will make sure that parents know what opportunities exist locally.

Key actions:
- By April 2009, we will publish a toolkit to help local authorities and service providers inform parents and children about local play opportunities;

- To ensure disabled children benefit fully from our investment in play, we have introduced funding requirements and are working with the third sector to provide expertise, advice and guidance for local authorities;

- New Sure Start Children's Centres will deliver best practice in design and provision of spaces for children to play; and

- The Building Schools for the Future capital investment programme will have clear requirements around outdoor play and recreational spaces in schools.

Children and playworkers in Nottingham City, one of the Play Pathfinders

The consultation response

Children and young people told us…

When asked who they thought could help them have more fun outside their home, 40% of children thought that schools could help by providing more after-school clubs, improving school playgrounds and taking them on trips.

When asked what they would like to see for 8–13 year olds where they lived, 44% of children said they would like to be able to use school grounds outside school hours.

Children said that we could make play more accessible to disabled children by:

- better designed provision where they can do the same fun things as everyone else;

- providing people around to help them;

- making sure they can get to play spaces easily;

- providing information about where the good play areas are; and

- making sure other children are aware of and respect their needs.

Adults told us…

When asked how schools can best support play, adult respondents suggested allowing access to school grounds outside school hours. Others said that schools should allow sufficient break times for young people to play, and that there should be improved training for school staff to highlight how best to meet children's needs for play.

Adults also wanted to see good quality outdoor equipment in schools, giving children access to different landscapes and varied spaces.

To support children with disabilities, respondents proposed: better access and safe routes; suitable equipment; more recognition that disabled children can join in mainstream settings with the right support; training for playworkers and funding for additional support staff; and toilets and changing facilities at play areas.

Respondents suggested that a range of groups of children have fewer opportunities to play, including: children from urban and deprived areas; Black and Minority Ethnic children; Gypsy, Roma and Traveller children; children whose first language was not English; children who are carers; children aged 13 and over; teenage girls; and children from rural areas.

Making sure all children access play opportunities

Informing parents

By April 2009, we will publish a toolkit to help local authorities and service providers inform parents and children about local play opportunities

4.1   Parents need to receive the best possible information about the play opportunities in their local area. Current Play Pathfinders and Playbuilders have already undertaken considerable work to consult with and inform their local communities about the development of new and improved play spaces.

4.2   By April 2009, we will publish a full toolkit of communications materials for local authorities to use in communicating to parents the benefits of play, as well as informing parents where good, safe play facilities are locally. The toolkit will be specifically designed to support local authorities in reaching the families of vulnerable children.

4.3   Pathfinders and Playbuilders will be able to select and adapt these centrally-produced communications materials to respond to local needs and the relevant stages of their play programmes.

4.4   We will also explore through the Play Pathfinders how parents can receive information from playworkers on what services and support they could receive from local children's centres and schools.

Additional work to support play for vulnerable children

4.5   There was a strong consultation response pointing to the need to do more to ensure that certain groups of children, often those that could benefit most, can take advantage of better play opportunities. We have set out how we will ensure play spaces are more available, accessible and inclusive for all children, as well as improving communications with parents and children about the services available.

4.6   Building on this, we are interested in exploring how we can do more to support children who are unable to take up opportunities to play. To inform our future work, we are planning to gather evidence to look at how vulnerable groups of children could benefit from extra support.

Play provision in prisons

4.7   The Prison Service has made considerable progress in encouraging family contact for prisoners and this has encompassed, amongst other things, the provision of play facilities for children visiting friends and relatives. There are now over 100 play areas for children in visits halls and with the assistance of third sector organisations many prisons provide supervised play activities, family days and family learning opportunities. The current development of specifications for delivery on the Children and Families of Offenders agenda across the Prison and Probation services will set minimum standards relating to play provision.

Opportunities for disabled children

To ensure disabled children benefit fully from our investment in play, we have introduced funding requirements and are working to provide expertise, advice and guidance to local authorities

Action to support play for disabled children

Capital investment: It is a requirement that the play spaces developed by local authorities with the £235 million capital funding must be fully inclusive and accessible for all disabled children and young people.

Supporting local delivery: Play England will be reviewing local authorities' plans and requesting evidence that they have consulted with disabled children. Local authorities who require guidance will receive support from the charity KIDS, and they can also use *Inclusion by Design: A guide to creating accessible play and childcare environments*[2], published by KIDS. We are funding KIDS to provide a senior full-time consultant to work with Play England, and local authorities where appropriate, to ensure our capital investment meets the needs of children with disabilities.

Engaging with parents and children: Play England have produced and are currently reviewing *Neighbourhood Play Toolkit* which provides information on how authorities can include disabled children in decisions about developing play spaces. Further information on this product is provided in Chapter 3, 'More places to play'. We are also developing materials for local authorities

4.8 Consultation responses from children and adults called for disabled children to be able to access the same play opportunities as every other child. In responding to these calls, we have also taken into account recommendations from Every Disabled Child Matters[1] (EDCM), a campaign group comprising Contact a Family, Council for Disabled Children, Mencap and Special Education Consortium. EDCM has

to help them communicate with parents and children, including those with particular needs.

Adventure Playgrounds: Play England have provided a briefing for Pathfinder authorities on adventure playground development stressing the inclusion of disabled children, including fully accessible toilets and other facilities. The design specification for these facilities will be included in the online technical guides Play England will set up on adventure playgrounds and playparks.

Training and development: As set out in Chapter 7, we will enable 4,000 playworkers to achieve an NVQ Level 3 by 2011. The National Occupational Standards have equality and inclusion issues threaded throughout each of the five mandatory and four optional units. Through their assessments, participants will be able to demonstrate their knowledge and understanding of the needs of disabled children and young people.

Measuring improvement: Chapter 7 provides details of the new national indicator for play for local authorities. This indicator will be informed by a TellUs survey which will enable us to find out the views of disabled children about the play provision in their area.

1   The recommendations are set out in: Every Disabled Child Matters (2008), *Going Places: ensuring the play and youth strategies deliver for disabled children and young people*, www.edcm.org.uk
2   Clare Goodridge and Philip Douch (ed) (2008), *Inclusion by Design: A guide to creating accessible play and childcare environments*, KIDS. www.kids.org.uk

Case study: Reaching disabled and vulnerable children in Rochdale

The Doorstep Project in Rochdale delivers play sessions directly to areas that have been identified as having little or no play facilities. The Council uses a designated lorry to bring play equipment and materials directly to the local areas where children need them most. This flexible approach allows playworkers to create a variety of exciting, inclusive and high-quality play environments in any local area, including in open spaces, fixed play areas and on the streets.

Through the project, the Council is able to provide tailored play sessions, for example sensory sessions for children with special educational needs, holiday playschemes for children with disabilities and sessions on encouraging community cohesion between minority groups. As a result, Rochdale has seen an increase in the number of vulnerable children enjoying play.

Case Study: Reaching Traveller children in Nottingham City

This project was set up by Nottingham City Play Service in 2002, with funding from the Children's Fund, to improve play provision for Traveller children at a site in Moorbridge in Nottingham City. In addition to providing high-quality play opportunities for Traveller children, the project has also built trust with the Traveller community, which led to some children also accessing mainstream provision in the area.

Traveller children have been encouraged to attend two play sessions each week at a local after school club, one of which is supported by the Traveller's playworkers. A majority of the Traveller children attend both sessions and also attend the Extended School programme as well as provision across the city. Their parents have also taken an active role in their children's play by providing transport and volunteering on trips.

welcomed our approach and will work with us going forward.

4.9　In addition to this, local authorities will be gathering the views of children and young people, including those with disabilities, as part of the national evaluation of the Pathfinder programme, which is due to commence early in 2009. Authorities will also be encouraged to conduct local surveys, based on Play England's local indicators that include participation and access.

Play and short break Pathfinders

4.10　Through the *Aiming High for Disabled Children* programme, the Government is providing local authorities with £269 million in revenue and £90 million in capital funding to invest in short break provision. Short breaks are an important service by which primarily disabled children and young people are temporarily cared for by someone other than their main carer. These breaks allow disabled children and young people to enjoy independent and valuable experiences, while also giving the carer time to rest or undertake activities they would otherwise be unable to achieve.

4.11 We have established joint play and short break Pathfinders – initially Enfield, Dudley and Sunderland – who will each receive support to coordinate their plans under the play and short break funding streams so as to enable greater opportunities for inclusive play provision for disabled children through public and voluntary and community sectors.

Improving play in the early years

Improving play through children's centres

> New Sure Start Children's Centres will deliver best practice in design and provision of spaces for children to play

4.12 Children's centres are service hubs where children under five years old and their families can receive seamless integrated services and information. Play is integrated into many of their services, for example, play sessions for children and their parents or carers, indoor and outdoor play areas and support for parents in encouraging play. Local childminders are supported by children's centres, including through access to resources such as toy libraries. Children with disabilities can access sensory play rooms in some centres.

4.13 Our national children's centre delivery partner, Together for Children, will ensure that local authorities link the roll-out of children's centres to other capital programmes. During the planning process for future children's centres, we will ensure that consideration is given to the extent to which the centre will provide sufficient indoor and outdoor play space.

4.14 Children's centre managers, playworkers and other children's centre staff also have a key role in informing parents, carers and others about the play resources located in the centre and in the local area.

Play within the Early Years Foundation Stage

4.15 The Early Years Foundation Stage (EYFS) is a statutory play-based early learning framework for maintained and independent schools and early years providers, which sets out the standards for learning and care and provides an entitlement to play-based experiences for every child aged birth to five.

Case study: Sensory play experiences in Greenwich

The Robert Owen Early Years Centre, a Sure Start Children's Centre in Greenwich has been working with a national charity, Learning Through Landscapes, to provide children and families with rich outdoor play experiences, incorporating sensory and environmental aspects to provide stimulating and meaningful play.

The outdoor play area has several distinct features which provide opportunities for child-initiated, structured and unstructured play and learning. A willow igloo encourages children's creative play, whilst a woodland walk promotes physical skills and activity. A vegetable patch enhances children's knowledge and understanding of the world through structured activity and a 'smelly' garden provides sensory experiences. Importantly, the provision of wet weather gear by the parents' group has meant that the play space can be used in all weathers.

4.16 In these settings, practitioners allow children the freedom to make their own choices about how and where they will play, joining in to encourage children to try out new ideas and activities. The EYFS places strong emphasis on meeting each child's individual needs and supporting progress at a pace that is right for them.

4.17 Alongside this, practitioners will plan and resource a challenging environment where they can support and extend children's play and observe how a child is developing so they can offer them tailored provision which meets the needs of every child and celebrates their achievements.

4.18 The EYFS states that, wherever possible, there should be access to an outdoor play area, and this is the expected norm for providers. In settings where outdoor play space cannot be provided, outings should be planned and undertaken on a daily basis (unless circumstances make this inappropriate, for example, if there are unsafe weather conditions).

4.19 The Department for Children, Schools and Families is committed to reviewing the EYFS in 2010. The overarching aim of this review will be to examine the requirements and guidance set out in the EYFS and to consider how well it has delivered against its objectives. Specific aspects of the EYFS that the review will examine include how well the EYFS promotes a high-quality physical environment that offers children a positive experience and the best opportunities to learn through play, including outdoor play.

Improving play provision through schools

4.20 The consultation responses from both adults and children showed that schools are considered to be important places for children to play, both in terms of play opportunities throughout the school day and in terms of making facilities available outside school hours.

New design guidance for schools

4.21 We have drawn together relevant materials and examples of good playground design to support school leaders and encourage them to further develop their play facilities. The materials are available at www.dcsf.gov.uk/play and we are encouraging school leaders, planners, designers and other interested parties to send us feedback.

21st century schools and extended schools

4.22 *21st Century Schools: A World-Class Education for Every Child*, published on 8 December 2008, sets out our vision for 21st century schools which focus on responding to the needs of a children and young people, their families and the wider community.

4.23 One of the key components of a 21st century school is the provision of a range of activities and opportunities to enrich the lives of children, families and the wider community. Providing access to the core offer of extended services, including play provision outside of school hours, is an important feature of this provision.

4.24 The Department will be consulting widely in order to build a strong consensus for the vision and for the way we will achieve it, leading to a White Paper on 21st century schools to be published in spring 2009.

School capital programmes

> The Building Schools for the Future capital investment programme will have clear requirements around outdoor play and recreational spaces in schools

4.25   We had a strong consultation response on the greater role school sites should have in supporting local play opportunities.

4.26   We have now introduced stronger expectations on play in the Building Schools for the Future (BSF) mandatory 'Strategy for Change' guidance and output specification. The national delivery partner for BSF, Partnerships for Schools (PfS), will promote these considerations to ensure local play services can be involved in school designs and headteachers and wider stakeholders fully understand how play is a key part of delivering our vision for 21st century schools.

4.27   In addition, Play England will be looking to make the best possible links between our play capital investment programme and BSF and Primary Capital Programmes, particularly in our Pathfinder areas. Where possible, we will enable local authorities to use play capital alongside other investment to promote out-of-hours and community usage of school play facilities.

4.28   The Department for Children, Schools and Families will work closely with PfS and Play England to monitor the impact of our new guidance and support work on the ground, and take stock of progress next year.

Play within the primary curriculum

4.29   The Children's Plan suggested that many children would benefit from a more gradual shift, from a play-based to a more formal classroom based curriculum, to reflect children's individual needs and differing levels of maturity. Research shows that the most effective pre-school settings (in terms of intellectual, social and attitudinal outcomes for children) were those in which there was a similar ratio of child-initiated activities to adult-led activity.

4.30   In January 2008, the Government asked Sir Jim Rose to carry out an independent review of the primary curriculum. The review has been asked to consider whether children would benefit if the Key Stage 1 curriculum, particularly in Year 1, provided more opportunities for exploratory play.

4.31   The interim report of the independent review of the primary curriculum was published on 8 December 2008, setting out its initial findings and provisional recommendations. The interim report suggests that children would benefit if the Key Stage 1 curriculum, particularly in Year 1, provided more opportunities for exploratory play. Recognising that some children starting primary education will be ready for more formal learning, the review is not proposing a rigidly uniform approach and suggests that teachers are best placed to make professional judgements on the balance to be struck between these pedagogical decisions. The review's final report and recommendations will be published in spring 2009.

Case study: Play throughout the school day in Hackney

Headteacher Louise Rosen, from St John Baptist Church of England Primary School in Hackney, believes that play is an important part of a good childhood and also important in raising standards within the school.

The school has embarked on an ambitious programme to develop exciting play spaces that can be used throughout the school day. Classrooms now extend into the playground, sheltered by a glass canopy; a sensory garden has been added, thanks to support from the Sunbabies Charity and the Linklaters law firm, and a play structure has been located within a huge sand pit. A huge adventure playground structure, complete with aerial walkways, cargo nets and a stage area, provides the main focus.

Teachers are able to use the gardens and play areas to integrate play within their topic plans right across the curriculum. Each Key Stage team works in partnership with a creative partner such as Circus Space, and an educational visit provides the stimulus for learning and play. School leaders worked closely with children in developing the new play areas, and children's enjoyment is reflected by their improved attendance and behaviour.

Play within the school day

4.32   In the *Fair Play* consultation, when asked how schools can best support play, around half of adults commented that schools should allow time for young people to play. Some respondents commented that the amount of time children had to play in schools was being eroded as both lunch and break times were being shortened.

4.33   There is an opportunity for the Government to explore research into how schools can best organise breaks and lunchtimes so that pupils are able to play. This may involve examining existing evidence on the extent to which children have time for play and recreation in school, and what pupils own views are on this in the context of schools promoting their wellbeing. This research may also involve considering the available evidence on the best approaches in terms of lengths of break times, and the benefits that can result.

St John The Baptist Church of England Primary School, Hackney

4.34 We will also explore the extent to which schools might find this information valuable and how far this information might impact on provision on the ground. We are clear that schools must have independence in deciding how to structure their timetables.

Inspecting play provision in schools

4.35 As part of the Children's Plan commitment to develop new school level indicators for pupil wellbeing, the Department for Children, Schools and Families and Ofsted are looking at how schools' provision for play can be identified and how this will feature in future school inspections.

Opportunities for young people

4.36 Young people should experience unstructured opportunities, as well as structured opportunities, to play through local provision. Where young people have choice and flexibility around their free-time activities, alongside a supportive environment, they may be more likely to become involved in positive community activities.

4.37 myplace was launched in April 2008 to deliver £190 million of Government capital investment to 2011 through grants of between £1 million and £5 million. Delivered by the Big Lottery Fund, myplace will provide world class youth facilities driven by the active participation of young people and their views and needs.

4.38 In addition, Chapter 6 provides details of other ways in which young people can access high-quality leisure facilities, such as through the Youth Opportunity and Youth Capital Funds and through Youth Taskforce investments.

Physical activity, physical education and sport

4.39 In the *Fair Play* consultation, we proposed taking steps to ensure that links are made at local level between school sports partnerships, County Sports Partnerships (CSPs) and play providers so that supervised play in particular is one possible means of engaging reluctant groups in more physical activity.

4.40 CSPs play a key role in co-ordinating local delivery and investment in physical activity, and in November 2008 the Department of Health announced their intention to support CSPs through an allocation of £1 million of funding in this financial year (2008/09). Chapter 7 further describes how health partners will support physically active play locally.

4.41 Linking to the wider PE and Sport Strategy for Young People (PESSYP), we are part funding a new programme designed to improve early learning for pre-school children in deprived communities through the provision of outdoor play areas with an emphasis on physical play. With Government investment and matched sponsorship, 10 pilot Playzones will be set up across the country to explore this area. The aim will be to evaluate these pilots and to replicate good practice across the network of school sport partnerships and early years providers.

Multi-skill Clubs

4.42 The Multi-skill Clubs (MSC) programme is an important part of PESSYP. MSC are now an established part of many high quality out-of-school hours programmes and are providing thousands of young people aged 7–11 with the opportunity to practice and perfect their fundamental movement and sport skills (such as running, jumping, skipping and catching), in a fun and challenging environment. They prepare young people for a lifetime of involvement in sport and physical activity and connect them to community sport clubs. It is aimed that there will be 3,600 MSC by 2011.

4.43 Currently there is a pilot to extend the reach of the MSC programme to young people aged 5–7. The pilot is due to report in summer 2009 and if successful will be considered for roll-out across the network of School Sport Partnerships.

Chapter 5
Playing safely

Childhood should be a time for enjoyment, learning and exploration, and it is everyone's responsibility – parents, practitioners, delivery partners, Government and children and young people themselves – to keep children and young people safe.

Children, young people and parents told us that concerns about safety are preventing children from going outside and accessing play areas, and that play facilities are often dull and are not challenging and stimulating for children. To address this, we will do more to tackle bullying and crime, improve road safety and increase the availability of appropriately supervised play, as well as to support partners to deliver safe and exciting play areas that children and young people want to see.

Key actions:

- We will publish guidance for practitioners on tackling bullying outside schools;

- We are taking steps to tackle youth-related crime through the *Youth Crime Action Plan* and the *Youth Taskforce Action Plan*;

- We are supporting links between local authorities, the third sector and community policing to improve appropriate supervision of children playing;

- Alongside this Strategy, we are launching pilot schemes to develop local models for volunteering to supervise children playing; and

- We are publishing guidance on proportionate risk management to support the delivery of exciting play spaces.

The consultation response

Children and young people told us...

The consultation asked children whether our plan to make play areas safer would make a difference, and 72% agreed. Children felt that safer places to play would:

- make them feel more confident about playing outside without fear of being bullied by older children, scared by traffic or bothered by strangers; and

- make their parents/carers feel happier about letting them play outside.

Children and young people raised the following issues:

- 42% of children believed that having adults around to look out for them would encourage them to spend more time outdoors.

- 57% of children responding to the consultation said they would feel safer about spending time outdoors if the roads were safer; and

- 55% of 8-13 year olds called for play spaces to provide more interesting and challenging things to do.

Adults told us...

Respondents said they would like to see more play rangers and more supervision, safer routes to play, cleaner play spaces, and action against bullying and crime. Respondents felt that the level of supervision children need depends on children's age and the context in which they're playing.

74% of respondents suggested a number of general traffic calming measures would allow children to play more safely in and around their streets and on the way to play areas.

A majority of adults said that children aged 8-13 needed play areas with more exciting equipment that let them take risks, and 91% of respondents believed concerns about being sued could lead to dull and unstimulating play areas.

Staying Safe

5.1   Staying safe is a fundamental part of *The Children's Plan*: children cannot enjoy their childhoods or achieve their full potential unless they are safe.

5.2   The Government published the *Staying Safe Action Plan* in February 2008, following extensive consultation. It sets out actions for the first ever cross-government strategy for improving children and young people's safety (underpinning Public Service Agreement 13), and it has been embraced by local authorities, the third sector and delivery partners as a major contribution to improving child safety.

5.3   The action plan covers all issues relating to the Every Child Matters outcome of 'staying safe', including keeping children safe from neglect and abuse, accidents, bullying, crime and anti-social behaviour and providing a safe and stable home environment.

Safeguarding children at play

5.4   Everyone working with children and young people, including those working in the play workforce either in paid employment or as volunteers, needs to be vetted to ensure they pose no threat to children and young people, and adults who support and supervise play should be alert to risks and indicators of harm and know when and with whom to share information to keep children safe.

5.5   To continue to make progress on safer workforce and safe employment practices, we committed to working with the Children's Workforce Development Council to roll out new guidance and training on recruitment for all of the children's workforce, building on the guidance and training that is already available for the school workforce. This is on track to be delivered by June 2009, and draft guidance is due for consultation in January 2009, followed by online materials in May 2009.

5.6   A number of organisations will help ensure children are safe, including children at play.[1] Following changes in Government legislation and the Children's Act 2004, every local authority now has a statutory duty to have a Local Safeguarding Children Board (LSCB), co-ordinating integrated, multi-agency responses to children's safety and welfare locally.

5.7   DCSF is undertaking a stocktake of LSCBs to develop recommendations that will help all LSCBs perform at the level of the best. The stocktake will be conducted in close collaboration with local authority and other partners and will report in 2009. To ensure that the reform to safeguarding that the Government set out in Every Child Matters is being implemented systematically, Lord Laming has been asked to prepare an independent report of progress being made across the country.

Local area accident prevention

5.8   We are undertaking a cross-Government Priority Review of Local Area Accident Prevention. The focus is on how local action to reduce unintentional injury in the under 18s can be better supported. The Review will conclude in December 2008 and its recommendations will be taken forward by the cross-Government Working Group on Child Accident Prevention, chaired by the Department for Transport.

Tackling crime and anti-social behaviour

5.9   Our consultation shows that youth crime and anti-social behaviour are concerns for many children and parents. Although some feel this is at times exaggerated or misrepresented in the media, a minority of young people do cause trouble and become involved in anti-social or criminal activities. It is important that we have in place strong actions that address unacceptable, anti-social or criminal behaviour. We also need to make sure young people at risk of offending get the right help to change their ways.

---

1   *The Independent Safeguarding Authority (ISA)* vets all individuals, paid and voluntary, who want to work with children and vulnerable adults. *The Child Safety Education Coalition* aims to increase access to out-of-classroom opportunities for children to learn about risk, safety and what to do in emergencies. *The National Safeguarding Unit for the Third Sector* will provide advice and assistance to third sector bodies on safeguarding issues. This unit will be up and running in early 2009.

Tackling bullying

> We will publish guidance for practitioners on tackling bullying outside schools

5.10 Building on the *Safe to Learn*[2] guidance for schools, we have committed to launch guidance, training tools and materials to support practitioners to tackle bullying which takes place outside of school, including around leisure activities and play. In October 2008, we appointed the charity 4Children to develop the guidance and materials, which we aim to launch in early 2009. We are exploring how best to support implementation of this guidance on the ground.

Youth Crime Action Plan

> We are taking steps to tackle youth-related crime through the *Youth Crime Action Plan* and the *Youth Taskforce Action Plan*

5.11 The Youth Crime Action Plan was published in July 2008 and sets out the Government's approach to tackling offending and re-offending by young people. It combines a series of short-term measures to make a tangible difference on the ground quickly with longer-term proposals to improve the operation of the youth justice system. The Action Plan takes a triple-track approach of enforcement where behaviour is unacceptable, support and challenge for those at greatest risk of offending, and early prevention to stop problems spiralling out of control.

5.12 Further information is available at: www.homeoffice.gov.uk/documents/youth-crime-action-plan

Tackling negative perceptions of young people

5.13 The consultation response told us that fear of groups of young people hanging around play areas prevents children from playing outside. Widely held negative perceptions of young people reinforce these fears, and there was a call for the Government to find opportunities to generate a wider awareness of the positive contribution young people make to their communities. Chapter 6 discusses this issue further.

Supervision of play

5.14 Responses to our consultation show a wide variety of views on who supervises children's play. This can range from a qualified playworker or a park ranger, to a 'friends of the park' management group, to community police patrols, maintenance staff or simply adults sitting in a café at a space designed for all ages. It is clear that there is some need to define the boundaries of responsibilities for play professionals, volunteers, local authorities and the police with respect to their roles in maintaining the safety of public space.

5.15 There was strong support for an emphasis on children and young people leading their own play, with endorsement of the principle that the supervisory role is to help create a secure atmosphere that encourages play in different ways, according to age, ability, culture, and circumstances.

2   Department for Children, Schools and Families (2007), *Safe To Learn: embedding anti-bullying work in schools*, www.teachernet.gov.uk/safetolearn

5.16 We are asking Pathfinder local authorities to explore local solutions to supervision. We expect them to consider and implement actions to increase supervision to improve the sense of safety, working with the third sector and across local services, including local police. We will collect evidence from this activity to support future guidance on play and to expand on the principles of supervision in a play context to ensure play is child-led.

Neighbourhood policing and play

> We are supporting links between local authorities, the third sector and community policing to improve appropriate supervision of children playing

5.17 It is important that those managing and supervising public space, including playworkers and volunteers, have good links with their local police and clear guidance on what to do in cases of criminal and anti-social activity.

5.18 Neighbourhood Policing is provided in all areas of England by teams of police officers and Community Support Officers. Neighbourhood police officers are readily accessible to work with local communities to identify local priorities and find solutions to local crime and disorder problems. To find your local neighbourhood policing team, see www.direct.gov.uk/neighbourhoodpolicing

5.19 We will explore models and best practice in joint working between neighbourhood police and the play sector through selected Pathfinders, to be identified jointly by the Department for Children, Schools and Families, Play England, the Home Office and the Association of Chief Police Officers (ACPO). Trials will run until summer 2010. We will then produce guidance for local authorities, police teams and others. A statement from ACPO supporting the Play Strategy is provided at Annex B.

5.20 All Pathfinder and Playbuilder authorities will be asked to ensure that all local organisations involved in play are aware of the role of neighbourhood police and that local police are involved in discussions on the development and supervision of local play facilities.

5.21 As we work with community policing to support play, a key element will be helping all professionals involved to understand the nature of unstructured play and what appropriate supervision may entail. Chapter 6, 'Child-friendly communities', highlights our new cross-professional training programme, which will include a specific module for professionals who supervise public space.

Case study: Community Policing supporting play in Exeter

In 2002, Parkswatch was set up to encourage Exeter's residents to become more involved with their local park and to encourage more children and young people to use the parks. It was established by Neighbourhood Watch, Devon and Cornwall Constabulary, Exeter City Council Parks and Open Spaces Department and Community Patrollers.

The group meets monthly to address issues relating to park usage, and provides a forum for parents and local residents to share views and work alongside young people to improve play provision in the parks. Parkswatch also provides activities for hard to reach communities, and local police have been involved in delivering a number of these activities, including cricket and football sessions. Children and young people have now returned to the parks, and parents are now more confident about allowing their children to play in the parks.

Volunteering

Alongside this Strategy, we are launching pilot schemes to develop models for volunteering to supervise children playing

5.22 In the *Fair Play* consultation, we committed to asking Pathfinder authorities to explore play volunteering schemes, with a view to developing proposals that could be replicated across the country.

5.23 We think that the most efficient approach is for the Government to collate learning on effective local approaches derived from Pathfinders, and then promote local take-up of this learning. The aim would be that play volunteering grows within current local and regional infrastructures, therefore supporting the local empowerment vision throughout our Play Strategy.

5.24 We are investing £1 million in Pathfinder pilots for play volunteering over 2008–11. These will research play volunteering models with a

Photo: Hannah Edwards

particular focus on supervision and community involvement. We intend to establish five pilots in total, covering a range of settings and themes, from urban and rural environments to different contexts such as adventure playgrounds, schools or street settings.

5.25　All Pathfinder local authorities will be expected to work in collaboration with their third sector and community partners, to examine issues such as recruitment, training, community ownership, sustainability, and incentives. Through the pilots we will look at these issues in depth, including trials of the new workforce qualifications for play (described in Chapter 7) as they apply to volunteers.

5.26　We are launching the first two pilots with our action plan, in Bristol and Rotherham local authorities. These will focus on youth and intergenerational volunteering in support of play. Details of these two pilots are provided at www.dcsf.gov.uk/play

5.27　A steering group is being established to advise on the volunteering pilots and other volunteering actions on play. This group includes:

- the national youth volunteering charity, **v**, whose local **v**involved team is supporting the Bristol pilot;

- the Centre for Intergenerational Practice, who are advising the pilot local authorities on the specific intergenerational details; and

- SkillsActive, the Sector Skills Council for the leisure sector, who are advising on volunteer standards and qualifications.

5.28　We are engaging further national volunteering organisations to become members of the steering group.

5.29　To support the action research pilots and the national advice of the steering group, we will also be collating other evidence through research, advice from sector partners and through our evaluation of the Play Strategy. This will provide a rounded picture from which we will develop proposals for national play volunteering by spring 2011.

5.30　Links to information on funding for the third sector are available from the Office of the Third Sector: www.cabinetoffice.gov.uk/third_sector/funding_finance_support/funding_finance_guidance.aspx

Case study: supervising play on the Wirral

Since 2003, the Wirral Play Council 'PlaySpaces' project has provided supervised play at parks, open spaces, streets and informal play spaces. Through the presence of playworkers, children aged five to 13 are now enjoying safer opportunities to play in these public areas.

The project works in partnership with organisations and individuals across the local area such as schools, Sure Start Children's Centres, park rangers, local community and resident groups, youth workers, the Community Safety Team and the police. The project is a borough-wide initiative that regularly supports a number of play sites, which are well attended by local children. Through the project, children are able to access a diverse range of healthy outdoor activities with the support of playworkers. Where, traditionally, groups of children from different areas would not play with each other, the presence of the playworkers has made it possible for different groups of children to enjoy playing together.

Safe routes to and from play

5.31 Road safety is a key concern in consultation responses. Great Britain has one of the best road safety records in the world but, while our overall child casualty rates are amongst the best, our child pedestrian fatality rates remain higher than in many other European countries. The Department for Transport (DfT) is delivering a range of initiatives[3] to improve road safety for children and published the Child Road Safety Strategy in 2007.

Designing streets and managing traffic

5.32 It is essential that local highways authorities and built environment planners take account of road safety in all environments where children are, including around schools, residential areas and play spaces.

5.33 It is for local authorities and not central government to decide what road safety measures are most suitable in their areas. To coincide with the publication of our Play Strategy, we have written to all local Directors of Transport about the importance of child-friendly road safety and planning measures that support local play opportunities. The letter can be found at Annex C.

5.34 In addition to their own resources, DfT provides funding to local authorities for road safety and other transport measures through the Local Transport Plan system. Since 2007, DfT has provided additional funding of over £100 million per year to replace (and exceed) the revenue previously received by safety camera partnerships.

5.35 A key expectation of our play capital building programme is that local authorities should develop safe routes and access to play spaces. Not only should this take account of the guidance and resources mentioned here, but should also take account of sustainable development and active travel. Sustrans, the sustainable transport charity, has provided guidance to all Play Pathfinder and Playbuilder authorities on how to ensure children and young people can enjoy independent and active access to play provision through its Active Play and Travel:

3   For full details, please visit www.dft.gov.uk/pgr/roadsafety/child

Tackling Obesity programme. This short checklist can be downloaded from www. sustrans.org.uk/play, and further guidance will be published by Sustrans early in 2009.

20mph zones

5.36 Our consultation showed significant support for more 20mph zones where children are playing. A properly planned 20mph zone, including effective speed reduction measures, is shown to substantially reduce casualty rates. DfT encourages the creation of 20mph zones where appropriate and has issued extensive guidance to local authorities. We encourage local authorities to implement properly planned 20mph zones around play spaces where possible.

5.37 The DfT's research project, *Local road safety evaluation and action learning,* includes a survey of some local authorities which will cover 20mph zones and other road safety issues. The three year project was commissioned in February 2008, with an interim report due in March 2009.

Road Safety Compliance consultation

5.38 In November 2008, the DfT launched a consultation on road safety compliance of road users. Responses are requested by 27 February 2009: www.dft.gov.uk/ consultations/open/compliance

Home Zones

5.39 Home Zones are residential areas with streets designed for very low vehicle speeds which better suit the needs of pedestrians and cyclists. They provide scope for social activities, such as children playing or chatting, to take place in street space formerly considered to be almost exclusively for vehicles. DfT has piloted around 60 Home Zones and produced good practice guidance for local authorities and developers. The pilots showed that traffic flows were significantly reduced, with the percentage of vehicles exceeding 20mph falling from 42% to 12%.

5.40 Sustrans is piloting a 'DIY Streets' project in 10 communities, developing innovative approaches to creating affordable Home

---

Case study: Ensuring safe routes for play

Cornwall County Council is a Playbuilder authority and is using the Sustrans checklist as part of the site selection process for Playbuilder investment and to identify where further work is needed to improve active and independent access to successful Playbuilder sites. The checklist has served as a focus for discussion between the Playbuilder implementation team and the Travel Awareness & School Travel plans team with the intention of joint working to survey children about how they travel to play areas and what improvements can be made.

In the **Bristol Pathfinder programme**, new lines of communication across play, transport planning and park services, is leading to a joined up approach between play area, green space and cycle route development. Cycle parking is now planned for most playgrounds across the city and a city-wide accessibility map is being generated that combines school, green space and play ground locations with paths, crossing points and bus stops.

Zone-type areas. A pocket guide and information sheet is available at www.sustrans.org.uk

Street planning guidance

5.41 DfT's *Manual for Streets* provides guidance for practitioners involved in the planning, design, provision and approval of new residential streets, and modifications to existing ones.

5.42 Quiet Lanes is a Countryside Agency initiative, which has the support of the DfT. Quiet Lanes are minor rural roads which are appropriate for shared use by walkers, cyclists, horse riders and motorised users.

Road safety resources for schools

5.43 DfT is developing a comprehensive suite of road safety educational materials for all age groups, to be rolled out over the next two years to schools. DfT is also promoting road safety training for children to improve their skills as pedestrians and cyclists, which will encourage more walking and cycling through improved confidence.

Photo: John Grimshaw/Sustrans

Cycling

5.44 Over the next three years to 2010–11, £140 million will be invested in cycling. This will include enabling an extra 500,000 children in

Year 6 to have access to Bikeability Training by 2012, as well as funding for more safe links to school via traffic calmed or traffic-free routes and supporting a number of Cycle Demonstration Towns around England, which will introduce a range of measures to encourage more cycling.

5.45 The National Cycle Network now passes within one mile of half of the population and as it continues to grow so does its popularity – over 354 million free walking and cycling trips were made on the Network in 2007 alone. The number of journeys will be boosted as Sustrans' Connect2 project to create a series of high-quality walking and cycling networks at 79 locations across the UK gets underway.

5.46 Over the next five years (to 2013), £50 million from the Big Lottery Fund will be matched with £100 million of other funding to enable people to make daily journeys to school, to the shops or the park without th eneed to get in the car. We are working with Sustrans to make effective links with roll-out of our capital programme in local authorities, in order to help children and families travel actively and safely to play areas.

Road safety publicity campaigns

5.47 As part of the THINK! Campaign, DfT launched a new road safety campaign, Tales of the Road, targeted at 6–11 year olds in November 2008, to raise awareness and understanding of the dangers of the road and to encourage safer road use. http://talesoftheroad.direct.gov.uk

5.48 DfT also launched the innovative Copycat campaign for parents in 2007 and will be producing a new teen safety campaign in 2009.

Safe travel on public transport

5.49 Where children and young people are using public transport, it is also important that their travel is safe. The Government is continuing to promote measures to improve personal security for public transport passengers, including:

- further guidance to Crime and Disorder Reduction Partnerships to encourage them to engage with the public transport sector;

- over 900 stations accredited under the Secure Stations Scheme, which is designed to establish and standardise good security practices;

- a forthcoming consultation on the tools and powers to tackle anti-social behaviour on public transport; and

- work with the Passenger Transport Executive Security Group to produce a forthcoming online toolkit to help practitioners tackle anti-social behaviour in bus travel.

Managing risk and providing exciting places to play

> We are publishing guidance on proportionate risk management to support the delivery of exciting play spaces

5.50 Children need to take risks to learn how to manage risks. This is an essential part of growing up, and play is one of the most important ways in which they develop this vital skill. Riding a bicycle, climbing a scramble net, or pushing a friend on a swing all involve risk. We cannot, and should not try to, remove all the risk from play.

5.51 It is essential to ensure that play managers and providers of play sites are aware of appropriate risk management. Risk management should be proportionate and realistic, taking into account both the benefits as well as the risks for children and young people to have exciting opportunities to play.

5.52 Alongside this Strategy, we are launching the *Managing Risk in Play Provision Implementation Guide*. This is non-statutory guidance, which has been endorsed by both the Health and Safety Executive and the Royal Society for the Prevention of Accidents. It shows how play providers can replace current play site risk assessment practices with an approach that takes into account the benefits to children and young people, including disabled children, of accessing challenging and exciting play experiences. We will be promoting this guidance across the capital programme. Details of how to order or download the *Managing Risk in Play Provision Implementation Guide* are available at www.dcsf.gov.uk/play

5.53 Effective approaches to managing risk are also covered in:

- the new *Design for Play* guidance on designing and building play spaces (see Chapter 3);

- the new communications toolkit for local authorities (Chapter 4); and

- the new qualifications for playworkers and cross-professional training for play-related professionals (see Chapter 7).

Addressing fears around litigation

5.54   From the consultation responses, we are aware of concerns that a fear of litigation is affecting the quality of play sites – children and young people often think sites are dull. We shall closely monitor the impact on local practice that our new *Managing Risk in Play Provision Implementation Guide* has and consider in due course whether any further action is needed to address unduly risk averse procurement for play sites.

Communicating the benefits and risks of play

5.55   In response to parents' feedback, the *Staying Safe Action Plan* committed us to launch a major new communications campaign on children's safety. This will build public understanding of child safety and how we can all take responsibility for keeping children safe and is backed by over £9 million over 2008–11. This communications activity will address the barriers to play, including parents' perceptions and understanding of the risks and benefits of play.

Chapter 6
Child-friendly communities

We want to see communities that give greater consideration to children's needs and interests – communities which are more child-friendly. Children and young people want their own views to be reflected in local decisions about how their neighbourhoods are designed and developed. In response to this, we are taking steps to make local areas more child-friendly and more welcoming for children, in particular, by working with local partners and the housing industry.

Key actions:
- We will ensure that children's needs are fully reflected in a forthcoming review of planning policy;

- New web-based guidance will bring together best practice for planning officers on supporting children's play and recreation;

- A new national partnership will deliver training to every local authority by March 2011, focused on helping the professionals who design and manage our neighbourhoods to understand the importance of play and child-friendly spaces;

- We are working with the social housing sector and regulators to ensure that play is supported in some of the most deprived areas;

- The Commission for Architecture and the Built Environment is working with the Government, local authorities, and the housing development industry to deliver residential developments and new housing growth areas that meet children's needs and interests;

- Our *Aiming High* strategy is taking steps to foster a more positive approach to young people across society.

The consultation response

Children and young people told us…

When asked how they would like to be involved if there was to be a new play area near where they lived, most children were keen to be involved in deciding where any new play areas were going to be (49%), choosing what would be in them (68%) and helping to build them (56%).

Children considered that, if they were fully engaged in the planning and design process, they could improve this by:

- choosing the equipment and facilities that they wanted to use and stopping adults from including things that children and young people did not like;

- ensuring that planners choose the right places to build new play areas so that they were near housing and that there were safe routes for children to access them; and

- making sure that play areas were suitable for disabled children.

Children felt that local communities could help them by being more tolerant, by not complaining about them playing near their houses and understanding that they were not being anti-social, for example by playing ball games.

Some children considered that people where they lived needed to be educated to understand that not all teenagers were yobs or 'hoodies' intent on anti-social behaviour.

Adults told us…

97% of respondents believed that it is important that communities are involved in the design of play spaces from an early stage. Respondents suggested gathering ideas from schools, from questionnaires and by asking local voluntary groups.

Some expert stakeholder respondents said that although the principal of involving children and communities in design was good, there must be a place for professionals who had experience, expertise, and vision.

When asked how parents and communities can support children playing outside, respondents suggested:

- communities could be more tolerant of children playing in and around their homes;

- parents could undertake volunteering opportunities in their communities;

- parents should act as good examples in the community;

- parents could share responsibility for supervising children between them; and

- parents needed to take more responsibility for their children's behaviour.

Respondents welcomed the proposal in the *Fair Play* consultation to counteract the negative perception of young people, including through:

- more positive stories in the media about young people;

- engaging children and young people in decision making as this would empower them; and

- getting young people together with older people to do more in the community.

A built environment more welcoming for children

Planning framework and guidance

> We will ensure that children's needs are fully reflected in a forthcoming review of planning policy

6.1   The need to consider children and young people's outdoor play and informal recreation is clearly set out in current Government planning guidance to planners and highways officers.[1] We will use the national planning policy review announced in the Communities and Local Government planning White Paper to assess the need to strengthen planning policy, or provide additional guidance, to help tackle obesity and support healthy communities. This review will ensure that children's play needs are considered appropriately.

> New web-based guidance will bring together best practice for planning officers on supporting children's play and recreation

6.2   We will also work with planning and highways officers, the Royal Town Planning Institute and other stakeholders to provide web-based guidance specifically relating to spaces and facilities for children and young people's play and informal recreation. This will be launched by Communities and Local Government in early 2009, and will help local authorities to develop effective local strategies for play space, bringing together various standards and good practice on child-friendly place making (shaping local

Considering plans for a new play site in Rotherham, as part of the area's Pathfinder programme

environment to reflect the needs of communities). In the interim, Play England will be issuing guides to help local authorities that need immediate advice.

6.3   The Department of Health is also currently developing a support package for planners, to help them to understand better the public health implications of planning. This will link into our wider work and the Play Shaper training programme that we are rolling out.

New cross-professional training to support play

> A new national partnership will deliver training to every local authority by March 2011, focused on helping the professionals who design and manage our neighbourhoods to understand the importance of play and child-friendly spaces

1   *Planning Policy Guidance 17: Planning for open space, sport and recreation (PPG 17)*, its companion guide, *Assessing needs and opportunities: a companion guide to PPG17*, and *Planning Policy Statement 3: Housing*. It is also recognised in the *Manual for Streets*, Department for Transport guidance to support the development of residential streets.

6.4   As proposed in *Fair Play*, we are now launching a programme of training to bring together the local professionals who have a role to play in making neighbourhoods more child-friendly. This new £3.2 million Play Shaper Training Programme will be delivered by a partnership made up of Play England, SkillsActive and Playwork Partnerships.

6.5   3,000 staff across all local authorities will be offered free training by 2011, starting with Play Pathfinder authorities in 2008-09. The programme's key aim is to enable a wide range of staff[2] to understand:

- the importance of play;

- their role and responsibility in supporting children's play and safe, active travel by children around their neighbourhoods;

- how play can help deliver other local priorities, for example increasing physical activity and developing sustainable communities; and

- what can be done to encourage children's play within available powers, drawing on good practice.

6.6   Alongside the launch of this publication, all Chief Planning Officers and Directors of Transport have received a letter highlighting the importance of planning that supports children's play, copied to their local authority's Chief Executive. This letter has been sent jointly by five Government Departments, and can be found at Annex C.

Residential areas and social housing
Social housing

> We are working with the social housing sector and regulators to ensure that play is supported in some of the most deprived areas

6.7   We estimate[3] that there are over 2.3 million children aged 15 or under living in social housing in England. These children will include those most in need of good, safe play opportunities that are free of charge, but unfortunately often live in deprived areas with low-quality public space.

6.8   Registered Social Landlords (RSLs) are therefore crucial local delivery partners for our Strategy, and are already making a

Photo: J Bewley/Sustrans

---

2   The audience for the training programme will those who plan, design and build houses and streets and manage green space, including private sector developers and registered social landlords; those who supervise public space, such as the police and parks staff; plus others who have a key stake in the play agenda such as public health practitioners and play workers.

3   Based on 2006/07 Survey of English Housing data

Case Study – informal play spaces in Islington

Islington Council has recently created informal play spaces for children within a safe external environment at Gambier House, a 20 storey tower block, in partnership with EC1 New Deal for Communities (NDC). Gambier House is managed by Homes for Islington and a Tenant Management Organisation, with a great deal of consultation and engagement being co-ordinated between the design team, who are also overseeing the implementation process, and the managing organisations.

The project has created a setting in which the residents are able to use the improved area for a variety of activities, for example to meet, eat, talk, play, sit, and garden. Rather than provide a large amount of fixed play equipment, the space provides a context in which residents can use the layout and structures as props and introduce moveable seats and toys.

Particular features appealing to young people have been located carefully, for example, a playful water feature as a meeting place near the entrance to the estate. In addition to this, at the outermost point on the site, furthest from the block but easily visible, there is a place designed to be attractive for young people to meet, talk, and play.

difference on the ground.[4] Social Landlords should be consulted in the preparation of Children and Young People's Plans in every local authority area and work in partnership with Children's Trusts to deliver on those plans.

6.9   The Government has established the Homes and Communities Agency (HCA) as the national housing and regeneration agency from December 2008. HCA has objectives to build and regenerate communities and to support communities in their continued wellbeing. A key aspect of this is the Agency's ability to provide community services, well-designed public realm, open space, green space, sports and play facilities to support communities as necessary.

6.10   The Government has also set up the Tenant Services Authority (TSA) which will be the regulator of social housing from December 2008. The TSA will consult widely in 2009 on proposals for new performance standards. These could include children's play issues where these are connected to social housing management. DCSF and Play England will respond to the consultation, and work with TSA to facilitate full consideration of children's play needs.

Building for Life

6.11   Building for Life is the national standard for well-designed homes and neighbourhoods.[5] The criteria state that functional and sustainable housing schemes should provide (or be close to) play and recreational areas.

4   The National Housing Federation (NHF) has recently published *iN business for neighbourhoods* which demonstrates the significant investment that Housing Associations across the country are making to provide play, informal sport facilities and landscaped areas. Housing associations are supported by the NHF through their published best practice guidance – *Standards and Quality in Development* (2nd ed)
5   Building for Life is run by a partnership between several national agencies, led by Commission for Architecture and the Built Environment (CABE) and the Home Builders Federation (which represents private home builders in England and Wales)

Funding from Communities and Local Government will support a nationwide network of 500 accredited assessors to enable new housing schemes to be evaluated against the Building for Life criteria.[6]

6.12   We will ensure that the Building for Life criteria and associated guidance appropriately reflect children's needs, and that the training programme for the new Building for Life assessors includes content on children's play.

New Growth Points

> The Commission for Architecture and the Built Environment is working with the Government, local authorities, and the housing development industry to deliver residential developments and new housing growth areas that meet children's needs and interests

6.13   There are particular opportunities to develop child-friendly communities in the New Growth Points and Growth Areas, where Government is working with a number of local authorities to increase housing stock in coming years.[7] Successful delivery of New Growth Points would contribute around 100,000 additional dwellings by 2016.

6.14   The design of these new housing developments provides an opportunity to include excellent child-friendly space. The Commission for Architecture and the Built Environment (CABE) is working with

Swainswick Explorers, a family-run service near Bath.
Photo: Play England

Communities and Local Government (CLG) to support Growth Points. We will work with CABE and Play England to ensure that specific input and advice on supporting children's play is available to these areas.

Green space

6.15   High quality green spaces are good for people and places. Children and families place high value on local parks as places to play, and our new national indicator asks children about their satisfaction with local provision. CLG is committed to improving the quality of parks and green spaces so that everyone has access to good quality green spaces, close to where they live.[8]

---

6   The assessors will also assist local authorities in completing their annual monitoring returns (AMRs): Government has recently included the Building for Life standard in its AMR core indicators for local and regional planning authorities

7   Announced in 2005, the New Growth Points initiative provides support to local communities. 29 areas were named as New Growth Points across the East, South East, South West, East Midlands and West Midlands

8   CLG's *Draft Urban Green Space Action Plan* outlines the aims to drive up standards in quality and increase access to and engagement with green spaces, and sets out the actions through which this will be achieved

6.16 A particular priority is improving the capacity of local authorities to drive improvements in parks through, for example, extra support in the development of green space strategies and recruitment and skills for the staff who manage and maintain green spaces. National data on green spaces is also being improved, and the green space database being launched in early 2009 will enable information to be shared across managers and the sector to help ensure good quality parks are accessible to the people that need them.

New opportunities in flagship developments

6.17 **Healthy Towns:** *Healthy Weight, Healthy Lives: a cross-government strategy for England* (published in January 2008) included a commitment to invest £30 million between 2008–09 and 2010–11 in a Healthy Community Challenge Fund (HCCF). On 10 November 2008 the Department of Health announced the nine towns that have been designated as Healthy Towns. These are: Manchester, Halifax, Thetford, Sheffield, Tower Hamlets, Tewkesbury, Dudley, Middlesbrough and Portsmouth.

6.18 These towns will build on existing work in their communities and test out their ideas on what further action needs to happen to make regular physical activity easier for their population. Several of the Healthy Towns have specific play-related projects.

6.19 **Eco Towns:** Eco Towns are a major opportunity for local authorities, house builders, developers and Registered Social Landlords to come together to build small new towns and to use this experience to help guide other developments across the country. Eco Towns offer an opportunity to create excellent play-friendly public space – incorporating the best in design and involving the community in the development and maintenance of play. Consideration should be given to routes to play space and opportunities for play in a range of locations, not just in parks or play areas. Those planning for and working in play in the proposed areas will have the opportunities to benefit from training and guidance available to local authorities.

6.20 **Olympics 2012:** We will hold a national event for Olympic planners and children's services departments early next year, hosted by CABE SPACE. This will explore how the development of the Olympic sites and wider local communities can support children's active travel and play; and consider how the Olympic legacy can further promote our long-term vision for play in every residential area.

Recognising and rewarding excellence

6.21 There are a number of schemes and awards that are currently used to improve standards and reward excellence in the design and management of public space.

6.22 A good example is the Green Flag Award Scheme, the national standard for parks and green spaces, which helps drive up quality across the country, as more spaces reach the standard every year. Communities and Local Government will continue to support this award and use the standard as a benchmark of quality. When assessing sites, Green Flag Award judges consider whether there is appropriate provision of facilities and opportunities for children's play. Since the Scheme's inception, the number of award winning green spaces in England has grown from seven in 1997 to 743 in 2008.

Exploring kite marks for child-friendly communities

6.23 Several national indicators can also be seen as measuring some of the component parts of what a child-friendly community might look like. There may be benefit in forming a basket of such indicators and standards, as a way to identify areas of excellence and share best practice.

6.24 We are interested in exploring the extent to which existing standards have an impact on provision for children, and will work with partners to include play-related indicators in existing standards and awards. If discussions with stakeholders indicate it would bring tangible benefits for children, we may then consider the establishment of a kite mark scheme to recognise excellence for child-friendly communities – covering both the built environment as well as positive social attitudes towards children playing in public spaces.

Public perceptions of children in public space

> Our *Aiming High* strategy is taking steps to foster a more positive approach to young people across society

6.25 As we said in *Fair Play*, to really make communities more child-friendly we need to do more than just change the built environment. We also need to work together as a society to create a culture that welcomes children in public space and challenges inappropriate 'No Ball Games' attitudes. This means adults being willing to share public space with children and understanding that it is often through play that children test boundaries and learn how to interact with others in their neighbourhood. But it also means children behaving responsibly, and that when they are playing children should respect other people and property, and that unacceptable and anti-social behaviour should not be tolerated. The statement from the Association of Chief Police Officers at

Case study: engaging communities in Knowsley

Knowsley became a Play Pathfinder in April 2008, and is placing a strong emphasis on putting communities, including children and young people, at the heart of planning play spaces.

Consultation has taken place at a wide range of events, including National Playday, festivals and flower shows, mobile play and play ranger sessions, primary schools and after-school clubs. The consultation team found it useful to use a variety of consultation methods, including: questionnaires and booklets; free play activities; graffiti walls; visits to unused spaces within their

areas; and showing examples of different play provision. A Local Play Audit (measuring the quantity, quality and accessibility of play spaces) and Local Needs Assessment also helped identify local needs and potential sites.

The authority is now considering options for sustainability in the future, including initiatives for volunteering, private sector partnership, social enterprise, developer contributions, covenants on new residential property in New Deal for Communities areas and support for community-led bids and projects.

Annex B reinforces the need for the right balance to be struck, so that children can have a legitimate stake in their neighbourhoods.

Giving young people positive things to do

6.26 Previous research and our *Fair Play* consultation does show that communities, children, and young people themselves are concerned about young people hanging around on the streets. We know that there is a genuine lack of facilities for young people, which is often cited as a contributory cause of anti-social behaviour. *Aiming high for young people: a ten year strategy for positive activities* set out the Government's vision for improving youth facilities in response to a clear ongoing

demand for more and better places for young people to go. **myplace** is a major Government programme to address this, as described in Chapter 4.

6.27 In addition, **The Youth Taskforce** has been created to help local services to deliver better opportunities for the most challenging and deprived young people and their families. £22.6 million capital investment has been provided to 50 local authorities to get facilities up and running quickly and open at the times young people and communities need them – Friday and Saturday evenings. This will be delivered alongside additional Youth Opportunity Funds (£25 million over

Designers in Rotherham look at plans for new play spaces as part of the area's Pathfinder programme

the next three years) that have already been allocated to the most deprived local areas to empower young people to have a real influence on activities in their area.

6.28 Chapter 4 describes how we will support greater levels of appropriate supervision of children playing, to ensure their safety. This supervision will also provide clear roles and boundaries on acceptable behaviour by children. By supporting supervsion through schemes for young volunteers, we will also help improve perceptions of young people through showing the valuable cotribution they make to communities.

Engaging with communities

6.29 In our consultation, adults and children demanded a greater say in the design and development of play space. We think that a powerful way for communities to appreciate better and accept children playing is to be closely involved in the decisions that are made around where play areas are, and how they are managed. Through local partnerships working to develop attractive play spaces where children, families and communities can enjoy time together in a positive way, we will foster better relationships between children, young people and communities.

6.30 Chapter 3 describes how we are ensuring this engagement happens through our local investment programme. And the next chapter shows how Communities and Local Government is putting in place strong new processes to ensure local people are given real control over local decisions and services.

Chapter 7
Embedding play in local priorities

Parents want play to continue to be a priority for the Government and local authorities and we also want to ensure that our investment will have a lasting impact. To achieve this we will create a policy framework and incentives for sustainable and effective delivery in every area and invest in a skilled workforce.

This will be driven by a shared understanding across local partners and local communities on the value of play, what good play opportunities look like and where they are needed, and what the various roles and responsibilities should be locally to deliver on this.

Key actions:

- We are introducing a new national indicator from April 2009 for local authorities, which will ask children how satisfied they are with their local parks and play areas;

- Updated statutory guidance for Children's Trusts sets out roles and responsibilities in relation to play;

- Jointly with Play England, we are publishing for consultation new draft guidance on how Children's Trusts and Local Strategic Partnerships can respond to children's play needs as they plan services and changes to neighbourhoods;

- We are working with the Department of Health to support active play as part of the drive by Children's Trusts to help children lead healthy lives, and through the healthy lifestyle campaign Play4Life;

- We are enabling 4,000 playworkers to achieve a level 3 playwork qualification by 2011;

- We are supporting the continuous professional development of leaders and managers in the play workforce by developing a new playwork management qualification; and

- We are investing £1.5 million in third sector-run adventure playgrounds and providing funding to help build third sector infrastructure that will support play locally.

The consultation response

Delivering the strategy on the ground

When we asked what needs to happen in order for the work we are suggesting on planning to make a difference on the ground, we received the following responses:

- 44% said it was important to get planners to understand play and what makes a good play area;

- 28% wanted more funding to be given to local authorities to improve existing facilities and to introduce new ones;

- 26% said that it was important to involve playworkers and other play professionals early in planning;

- 12% said that access to funding should be made easier for community groups and organisations; and

- 6% wanted more funding for playworkers at play areas.

Local priority-setting: a higher profile for play

Our consultation asked how we can ensure that play is given a high priority by local areas. Key responses included:

- 32% suggested legislation or the introduction of compulsory play strategies;

- 31% stressed that it was important to have funding ring-fenced to allow local authorities to deliver the Play Strategy;

- 29% thought it would be beneficial to have a positive media campaign, to show people the benefits of play; and

- 27% said that it was important that local authorities were given sustained funding to maintain play areas and equipment.

The role of the health sector

95% of respondents said Primary Care Trusts could promote healthy play by informing communities about the importance of play. Respondents also noted potential links between the Play Strategy and the Government's strategy to reduce obesity in young people.

The role of playworkers

- 53% of respondents recognised that playworkers have a crucial role. Respondents said that playworkers could enhance the play opportunities for children and young people and help educate parents.

- 30% were of the opinion that the playwork profession currently had a low status and that playworkers were currently undervalued. They welcomed the plans to improve the status of playworkers through qualifications and improving pay prospects.

- 14% said that playworkers should organise fun activities and should offer more outdoor adventurous play for children and young people.

- 14% suggested that playworkers could simply remind children how to play and encourage them to play spontaneously.

- 12% said that an important role for playworkers was to provide supervision so that children could feel safe when playing.

Play within Departmental priorities

7.1 The Children's Plan set out a vision to 2020 to make this country the best in the world for children to grow up in, and play is a key element of that vision. Within the Department for Children, Schools and Families, we have positioned play firmly within our first Departmental Strategic Objective. Play has been embedded across the delivery planning for Public Service Agreement (PSA) 12 on child health and wellbeing. We are ensuring that children's play needs are appropriately reflected across a range of other Government PSAs. We have also ensured that the Government Offices will support play regionally and locally.

Embedding play in local government thinking

7.2 Local councils have always provided facilities to support children and young people's play and leisure. The strong emerging evidence on the wide benefits of play, and the clear strength of public feeling on local play opportunities, will make Local Strategic Partnerships want to consider further the profile they currently give to outdoor play facilities in their decision-making. Good play opportunities can improve communities' quality of life, and developing them is a proven way to engage with local people. As such, local play provision should be thought of in the context of the local authority's place making role to create sustainable communities.

A national indicator for play

We are introducing a new national indicator from April 2009 for local authorities which will ask children how satisfied they are with their local parks and play areas

7.3   From April 2009 the National Indicator Set will include indicator NI199, showing what local children think about the parks and play areas in their local area. This will be measured through the TellUs survey of school-aged children, and will be reported against by Ofsted for every top tier local authority as part of the annual Comprehensive Area Assessment (CAA) process.[1]

7.4   In our baseline data from the 2008 TellUs 3 survey, 45% of children rated parks/play areas as 'very good' or 'fairly good'. However, too many children were indifferent about their local parks and play areas, or rated these as poor.

7.5   Looking forward, we want to see at least 100,000 more children telling us every year that their local play areas and parks are good or very good. This will be the progress we will measure to show us that children and young people are enjoying better play opportunities. Progress will be measured by pupils' responses to the TellUs survey as well as in the evaluation of the Play Pathfinder and Playbuilder programmes.

7.6   We want to see progress across every local authority in the country. Where local authorities are shown to have relatively low levels of child satisfaction with local play facilities, we will ask the authority and Government Office to consider whether NI199 should be considered as a local target, including within the Local Area Agreement.

7.7   The Government will also analyse the contribution that lay makes towards other indicators within the Local Area Agreements, and we will share this mapping with local partners, to highlight how integral play is to children's and community services.

Children's Trusts and play

Updated statutory guidance for Children's Trusts sets out roles and responsibilities in relation to play

7.8   New statutory guidance for Children's Trusts on inter-agency co-operation to improve the wellbeing of children, young people and their families has been issued. The guidance describes how the neighbourhoods in which children live should be accessible to them by foot and bike, and provide a range of high quality opportunities for play and recreation. When considering children's safeguarding needs, Children's Trust partners should consider traffic calming measures, access to quality green spaces and providing sufficient opportunities for safe, outdoor play and safe places for teenagers to meet.

7.9   This will require a strategic approach to play across the local area, with the full involvement of children, local communities

---

1   Comprehensive Area Assessment (CAA) will replace the Comprehensive Performance Assessment (CPA), Children's Services Joint Area Reviews, Annual Performance Assessment of services for children and young people and Social Services star ratings from April 2009. CAA will be a more risk-based, forward-looking approach that will focus more on the delivery of outcomes for the area than on the performance of individual institutions

and the third sector in decision-making. Delivering excellent outdoor play opportunities for all children will require working closely with the broader Local Strategic Partnership on issues such as town and highways planning and the management and maintenance of public space, in order to promote communities that are more child-friendly.

7.10 Subject to legislation to extend ownership of Children and Young People's Plans (CYPPs) to all statutory partners, new regulations for CYPPs are expected to come into force in spring 2010. It is planned that consultation on revised guidance to accompany the CYPP regulations will be circulated in autumn 2009. This will contain a clear message that assessments of local play needs should be considered, and play and recreation organisations should be consulted, in the development of the plans.

New guidance on local strategic planning

Jointly with Play England, we are publishing for consultation new draft guidance on how Children's Trusts and Local Strategic Partnerships can respond to children's play needs as they plan services and changes to neighbourhoods

7.11 To support Children's Trusts and Local Strategic Partnerships in delivering on these responsibilities to improve provision for children's play, we are issuing for consultation non-statutory guidance, *Implementing the Play Strategy*. This is intended to help senior local managers in their strategic planning and will support performance on the new national

indicator NI199. This guidance will also help local authorities build upon the Play Strategies they already have in place through the Big Lottery Fund's Children's Play Initiative, and meet requirements under the terms of their Children's Plan funding to embed investment within strategic planning around play. The draft guidance will be available at www.dcsf.gov.uk/consultations

District Councils

7.12 In two-tier areas, district councils have an important large role in delivering play opportunities, particularly in respect of community-based facilities in rural areas. The new statutory guidance for Children's Trusts emphasises that district councils should be fully engaged and are fully accountable for services in which they have an interest. Through our capital programme, we are requiring that district (and parish) councils are fully involved in decision-making around the new investment.

Supporting active play

We are working with the Department of Health to support active play as part of the drive by Children's Trusts to help children lead healthy lives, and through the healthy lifestyle campaign Play4Life

7.13 Active, outdoor play is a key area of interest for public health services locally.[2] The cross-Government strategy *Healthy Weight Healthy Lives* emphasised the role that active play and travel can have on children's weight. All Primary Care Trusts (PCTs) are required to have a plan in place for tackling obesity in under 11s; and 130 local authorities have

2   The Chief Medical Officer advises that children and young people should achieve a total of at least 60 minutes of at least moderate intensity physical activity every day. At least twice a week this should include activities to improve bone health, muscle strength and flexibility.

Case study: Creating a Play Partnership in Gateshead

Gateshead began to discuss establishing a Play Partnership in 2005, and the Gateshead Children's Trust Development group initially convened a cross agency group including the voluntary sector. This group drew up a 'First Steps Play Strategy', which outlined principles for play in Gateshead, and a plan to establish a Partnership.

The Gateshead Play Partnership was set up from the nucleus of this group. Service providers from the play, early years, leisure, youth and school sectors were invited, but also representatives from right across the Council, regional training providers and play organisations. Since

Gateshead Council adopted a Play Strategy in March 2007, the Partnership now meets three times a year, and the representation services from the council have been invaluable. A Play Strategy Executive Group, drawn from the full Partnership, now meets monthly to progress a Play Action Plan.

The members of the Play Partnership were very clear that they wanted to be independent, while acknowledging the positive role of the Council in developing play opportunities. The Partnership now provides the forum for discussion and debate and steers play matters in Gateshead.

prioritised child obesity in their Local Area Agreement or local targets. This provides huge incentives for a new focus by Children's Trusts on supporting active, outdoor play.

7.14 The new statutory guidance for Children's Trusts describes how to make a reality of the key partnership between local authorities and PCTs that will deliver on their joint agenda. This covers Joint Strategic Needs Assessment, joint development and sign-off of local Children and Young People's Plans (CYPP), and budget transparency, setting out the contribution of the PCT to implementing the CYPP and an agreed process in each locality for aligning or pooling budgets.

7.15 Play England is conducting a three-year play and health research project, funded by the Department of Health. The project will investigate parental and child concerns about active play, and how to encourage families to get children playing.

Case study: Partnership between health and play services in Halton

Halton Borough Council has invested significantly in modern, stimulating play facilities over the last 10 years and recognises the impact that play has on improving children and young people's health. To build on their investment in play, the borough and St Helens Primary Care Trust (PCT) have created an innovative partnership in which the PCT has agreed to fund a team to maintain new play facilities.

The PCT will fund an additional two person Playground Maintenance Team, at a cost of £80,000 per year for at least five years, and in return the Halton Borough Council will create five new play facilities. The PCT believes that health services should place an emphasis on health promotion, wellbeing and illness prevention, as well as treating illness. It is therefore keen to work with partners and the public to better improve lifestyles, including through supporting play.

Play4Life

7.16 Change4Life is a new £75 million initiative backed by the Department of Health that aims to help every family in England eat well, move more and live longer. A major advertising campaign will appear from January, and a website www.nhs.uk/change4life will provide help, advice and support for parents.

7.17 Play is a clear contributor to the Change4Life programme and a great way to encourage children to have a more active lifestyle. A number of sub-brands have been developed as part of Change4Life, including Play4Life. Play4Life can be used by any organisation to promote play related programmes and initiatives. We will explore how Play4Life can be embedded in the delivery of this Play Strategy and implemented at a national and local level.

Enabling communities to drive a greater focus on play locally

7.18 The previous chapter described how Communities and Local Government's (CLG) White Paper *Communities in Control: real people real power* offers a blueprint for how communities can be given real control over local decisions and services, providing opportunities to influence children's services and play facilities. Given the strength of public opinion on local play facilities, we see this as an important way in which play's profile can be raised in local government priorities.

7.19 The White Paper identifies a duty on local councils to involve local people in key decisions which will come into effect in April 2009, and a new duty to respond to petitions, so that when local communities put forward proposals for action to improve play space, their proposals are properly debated and responded to clearly. Play England's work to support community engagement in local play projects and play strategies will make full use of these new opportunities, and signpost the significant new Office of Third Sector and CLG funding that is available to support community empowerment and community-led projects.

7.20 Recognising that young people need genuine influence over local services, CLG have also funded the Young Advisor Charity to support the growth of over 300 Young Advisors nationally. Young Advisors have been trained as consultants to guide local authorities and other local partners about what it is like for a young person to live, work, learn and play in their neighbourhood.

Case study: Community empowerment in Torbay

Indigos provides free, open access play on an urban woodland site for children of all ages in Torbay. Activities for children and young people include building dens, making fires, cooking, growing plants and climbing trees. The service was started by a group of local parents in an area of Brixham with higher than average levels of deprivation and few opportunities for children and parents to meet and socialise.

The group of parents identified and cleared a derelict wooded site adjacent to a local school, working with children and young people. The group negotiated a 25-year lease with Torbay Council for the land and have secured funding from a number of sources including the Big Lottery Fund, Extended Services, the Local Network Fund and Living Spaces. The group will aim to secure further funding when this ends. In addition to six members of staff, there are six volunteers who are mostly parents, and new parents and community members are always encouraged to support the project.

National learning

7.21   A national evaluation of the Play Pathfinder and Playbuilder programmes is being carried out by SQW Consulting and Ipsos MORI to show how improvements to local play facilities impact on children, families and the wider community. This will include gathering evidence on: children's satisfaction with and use of local play areas; parents' attitudes towards play; how better play opportunities might help improve children's wellbeing; how improvements affect the wider community in terms of community

involvement/cohesion; and how play is integrated into local authorities' planning and delivery of services.

7.22   The evaluation will collect information on these outcomes before and after play improvements are made so we can see what difference the investment has made. Interim reports of findings will available in 2009 and 2010, with the final report following in 2011.

Local needs analysis and evaluation of progress

7.23   We think it is important to help local partners to be able to effectively map play provision in their areas, and also to be able to assess the quality of that provision to inform future planning. To support needs analysis and resource allocation, Play England will develop by February 2009 a national system and methodology for collating local information on play spaces, and will compile a new national database.

7.24   To support local data on the new play indicator NI199, all Play Pathfinders and Playbuilders are being encouraged to undertake local evaluation to assess the impact of the capital investment programme. Our national evaluators will support local authorities in this task by sharing data, learning, research tools and evaluation expertise.

7.25   Play England will provide day-to-day support to authorities as they undertake their local evaluations. Play Pathfinders and Playbuilders may wish to use specific play indicators developed by Play England for their local evaluations (detailed guidance on

the play indicators can be found at:
www.playengland.org.uk).

Building the play workforce

7.26 The Children's Workforce Development
Council (CWDC) is leading the programme of
work to deliver the Children's Plan
commitments to further professionalise the
workforce who support and supervise play.
Working with partners, including SkillsActive
and the Learning and Skills Council, CWDC is
making good progress. We will continue to
work with sector leaders to ensure the play
workforce is well supported.

> We are enabling 4,000 playworkers to achieve a
> Level 3 playwork qualification by 2011

7.27 A delivery and funding model has been
agreed to fund the Level 3 National
Vocational Qualification (NVQ) in Playwork
through the Learning and Skills Council's
Train to Gain programme, and CWDC has
agreed to fund training providers to deliver
the Level 3 Award in Playwork for Early Years
and Child Care Workers.

7.28 There is clear enthusiasm within the sector
to increase professionalism throughout the
workforce, and playworkers are now
beginning to benefit from this investment
in their skills development. We expect rapid
progress to be made towards the 2011 target
of 4,000 qualifications achieved.

Playworkers and children in Nottingham City

Case Study: A playwork graduate

James Jeffrey graduated from the Playwork Sector Endorsed Foundation Degree, validated by the University of Hertfordshire, in July 2008. This qualification is designed to be flexible and practice focused, and is aimed at both learners wishing to enter the profession and well as those seeking continuous professional development. It includes a substantial work-based learning element, and covers a broad range of play and playwork theory and practice.

James says: 'It was really good to be able to discuss my own ideas about play with people from different backgrounds. It was also useful to look at business planning and project management. This has helped me articulate my ideas and explain to others what needs to be done. Having the qualification has made me more respected as a professional. It gives you confidence that you know what you are doing and gives you more evidence to support it.'

By studying part-time, James was able to continue his employment as a play development worker with Stevenage Borough Council. After graduating, James has now gained a new role as the lead on the Council's Play Out Project, which offers free play activity sessions to children after-school and in the school holidays.

We are supporting the continuous professional development of leaders and managers in the play workforce by developing a new playwork management qualification

7.29 A new development programme for leaders and managers of front line staff in playwork settings is currently being designed. We expect this to be a graduate level programme, of around seven to 10 days' duration, which will focus on enhancing professional skills, knowledge and understanding in management and leadership in a playwork context.

7.30 The content of the programme is being developed through a national steering group, who will also look at how the learning can be accredited. We expect the programme will be ready to deliver in 2009 to an initial phase of 200 playwork managers.

Research into graduates' deployment within the play workforce

7.31 SkillsActive will explore how graduates may most effectively be deployed within the playwork workforce and add maximum value to the sector. The study is expected to identify models that could be used to underpin the training and development of graduates within the sector. There will be fieldwork and consultation followed by a final report early in 2009, which we will then consider.

Ensuring playworkers are part of integrated services locally

7.32 We will work with CWDC and partners to look for ways to enhance the ability of playworkers to support joined-up local services. A key consideration will continue to be helping playworkers to understand the importance of assessment of early identification and referral for any additional needs that a child may have.

Quality in Play

7.33   Quality in Play is a quality assurance system developed by playwork practitioners for school-age play and childcare provision, robustly tested through a pilot programme to ensure it was fit for purpose across a range of play providers. Growing numbers of play providers across the country have used it to raise standards and demonstrate quality play provision. It is now being rolled out nationally by Play England, in support of the Play Strategy's aims.

The role of the third sector

7.34   The third sector is already a significant local provider for play, and the responses to the consultation called for further support to build the third sector. An effective local third sector body can act as a strong champion for play in local authority business, and a channel for engaging communities and supporting volunteering. However, we recognise that many third sector play organisations have concerns about attracting funding.

7.35   Significant funding is being made available from the Office of the Third Sector to support the third sector, including the £130 million Grassroots Grants and £70 million Communitybuilders programmes. Play England will be signposting this as they work with local authorities.

7.36   We aim to see a greater role for the third sector in the longer-term delivery of our vision, and in our capital programme. We plan to work with the play third sector to carry out a review of their value-added, capacity and sustainability.

Glamis Adventure Playground, led by Play Association Tower Hamlets. Photo: *Play England*

New support for local, third sector play provision

We are investing £1.5 million in third sector-run adventure playgrounds and providing funding to help build third sector infrastructure locally

7.37 This funding will be made available from April 2009 to help refurbish existing third sector-run adventure playgrounds, which provide important play opportunities to some of the neediest children. Further details of how we will manage this funding will be released shortly.

7.38 In Chapter 3, 'More places to play', we also announced additional support via Play England to develop third sector play infrastructure locally, in order to enable communities to be fully involved in the improvements to their play areas.

Involving business

7.39 Businesses and employers are already contributing to play provision in a range of ways – from the Sainsbury 'Active Kids' campaign to business partnerships with voluntary sector organisations working with young people, to teams of volunteers helping to refurbish facilities. We will learn from existing good practice to help more businesses find out about how they can get involved.

Glossary

Adventure playground: An open access play setting staffed by trained playworkers where children can find materials and support to build and adapt their play space, have fun and take managed risks in a safe environment. They will normally have indoor facilities and are often located in high-density urban areas, where other safe outdoor play opportunities in parks and green spaces will be limited

Adventure playpark: shares many characteristics with an adventure playground, but will be part of a wider park or green space and will often support a range of family activities

CABE: The Commission for Architecture and the Built Environment

CLG: Communities and Local Government

Community: Sustainable communities are places where people want to live and work, now and in the future. They meet the diverse needs of existing and future residents, are sensitive to their environment, and contribute to a high quality of life. They are safe and inclusive, well planned, built and run, and offer equality of opportunity and good services for all

DCMS: The Department for Culture, Media and Sport

DCSF: The Department for Children, Schools and Families

DfT: The Department for Transport

DH: The Department of Health

Neighbourhood: Geographically localised community

Open access: Staffed play provision where children can come and go as they wish

Play: What children and young people do when they follow their own ideas and interests in their own way and for their own reasons, balancing fun with a sense of respect for themselves and others

Play area/space: A free and accessible space that provides unrestricted opportunities for play and informal recreation for children and young people. Play spaces include equipped playgrounds, kickabout areas, adventure playgrounds and skateparks

Play ranger: Detached playworkers, or 'play rangers', travel to specific sites in communities at advertised hours to bring play opportunities to children and families, often involving volunteers

Playground: The area provided by a school for children to spend their breaktimes

Playworker: Playworkers plan, organise and oversee part in play and leisure activities for children. They work in various settings, such as adventure playgrounds, after-school clubs and holiday playschemes. Their work could involve activities ranging from art, crafts or drama, to taking children on outings, and from cookery to outdoor games. They specialise in enabling play to be child-led, whilst providing rules and boundaries around behaviour

PSA: Public Service Agreement

Third sector: Voluntary and community groups, social enterprises and charities

Annex A
Play Pathfinder authorities

First 20 Play Pathfinders

The first 20 local authorities to become Pathfinders were announced in April 2008:

East of England
Cambridgeshire

East Midlands
Nottingham City

London
Hackney
Tower Hamlets
Camden
Enfield
Kensington and Chelsea

North East
Sunderland
North Tyneside

North West
Knowsley
Blackburn
Rochdale

South East
Portsmouth
East Sussex

South West
Bristol
Bath and North East Somerset

West Midlands
Wolverhampton
Dudley

Yorkshire and The Humber
Rotherham
East Riding

Final 10 Play Pathfinders

Alongside this Strategy, we are now announcing 10 final Pathfinders:

East of England
Luton

London
Lambeth
Merton

North East
Newcastle

North West
Wigan
Blackpool

South East
Oxfordshire

South West
Cornwall

West Midlands
Sandwell

Yorkshire and The Humber
Kirklees

Annex B
Endorsements from stakeholders

The Association of Directors of Children's Services

"The ADCS very much welcomes the Government's new Play Strategy. The Strategy will help local authorities, their partners and communities to transform public parks, children's play areas and school grounds so that all children have the opportunity to enjoy playing outside with their friends in a safe, stimulating and exciting environment."

The Local Government Association

"The Local Government Association welcomes this Play Strategy. Providing positive and stimulating places for children to play has always been an important aspect of the work of local authorities. From adventure playgrounds to support for voluntary sector play centres and out-of-school provision, local authorities have played a leading role in the development of play opportunities for children.

"Improving and extending children's play areas and making neighbourhoods more child-friendly – creating places where children can thrive – is not only good for children; it is good for their families and communities too.

"England's councils take play very seriously. We need to raise the profile of play and those who work in play. The Play Strategy highlights the crucial opportunity for local authorities to develop play opportunities as part of their integrated strategy for children. It reinforces that local government will continue to do all it can to support play and encourages the play sector to work with it to take full advantage of the opportunities offered. It should enable councils to work with other agencies and with children and families themselves to make play come alive in the best way possible for them and their communities."

The Association of Chief Police Officers

"The Association of Chief Police Officers (ACPO) is pleased to support the Government's Play Strategy. An environment that is welcoming and accepting of children and young people playing sociably and respectfully outside and meeting their friends is the sign of a healthy community. Importantly, the Play Strategy recognises there is an appropriate balance to be struck between meeting the developmental needs of children and young people through free play without being over-supervised and the need to ensure they are safe and protected from crime and anti-social behaviour.

"ACPO recognises the potential tensions and misconceptions within communities regarding groups of children playing on the streets and in open spaces and the need to manage this. Children and young people often gather in groups and it is important to recognise their right to associate with their friends and to play, so long as this is within acceptable boundaries of behaviour and they do not prevent other members of the community, including other young people, safely enjoying shared public space. Crime and anti-social behaviour will not be tolerated.

"ACPO will work with partners involved in the Play Strategy to maximise its integration with neighbourhood policing approaches, and will write to police in play pathfinder authorities to encourage them to get involved in planning at the local level and to support local outcomes. Approaches to children and young people in this context will need to raise awareness of what is acceptable behaviour and what is anti-social behaviour and, wherever possible, finding solutions to local issues through community dialogue and conflict resolution between children, young people and other local residents. ACPO is pleased that the cross-professional training being developed through the Play Strategy will provide support for local police to improve skills and aid better communication with children and young people of all ages."

The Sustainable Development Commission

"The Sustainable Development Commission welcomes the new Play Strategy and the encouragement it provides for Children's Trusts and Local Planning partners to create child-friendly spaces. We are particularly pleased by the focus on reducing barriers to play caused by road traffic, and also welcome the promotion of green and natural spaces as places which offer children a range of physical and psychological health benefits, and foster their understanding of nature."

The Commission for Architecture and the Built Environment

"At the Commission for Architecture and the Built Environment (CABE), we strongly believe that professionals working in planning, design and

management must come together in a combined effort to create successful, well-designed neighbourhoods. CABE welcomes the Government's Play Strategy and urges local authorities to be creative and imaginative in taking it forward. It should lead to a much more holistic, creative and collaborative approach to the design of play space, led by professionals with the appropriate range of skills, knowledge and experience. Children need to be put at the heart of the planning and design of public space. By integrating more playable spaces into the public realm, a more child-friendly environment can be created that meets the needs of the wider community and is fun for all."

Town and Country Planning Association

"Planners have a crucial role in the design of our public realm, which includes spaces suitable for play and informal recreation. We welcome the support outlined for planners to consult local communities, especially children, when creating play areas. Involvement must mean being lead by children, as with best play schemes, recognising that young people need genuine influence over local places and services."

Department of Health

"Play is essential for healthy physical, psychological and social development. Fortunately, play is what children do best. Running around, having fun with their friends and burning off energy is a great way for youngstres to step up to 60 minutes of physical activity every day."
Sir Liam Donaldson – Chief Medical Officer

Royal Town Planning Institute

"The Royal Town Planning Institute commends this Strategy as mapping a road towards healthier, happier and more sustainable communities."

Annex C
Letter to Chief Planning Officers and Directors of Transport

Child-friendly public space and transport

The purpose of this letter is to draw your attention to the first national **Play Strategy for England** which has been published today, and to set out the role Government would like you to take in supporting its local delivery in the context of Planning Policy Guidance 17; Planning Policy Statements 1, 3 and 12; the Child Road Safety Strategy; and PSA13 – to improve children and young people's safety.

See www.dcsf.gov.uk/play. Chapters 5 and 6 of the Play Strategy will be of particular interest to Chief Planning Officers and Directors of Transport.

Extensive consultation over the summer has told us that better and safer opportunities for children's active, outdoor play and recreation in public space are a priority for local people. New evidence demonstrates not only the range of benefits for children's health and wellbeing these can bring, but also the wider beneficial impact that more child-friendly built environments and transport can have on public health, residents' satisfaction with their local area as a place to live, social capital and cohesion, and sustainable community development.

The Play Strategy recognises that planning and wider local place shaping is of fundamental importance to the quality of space available for children to play, and to the ability of children to access that space safely by foot and bike. We have consulted widely with planners, highways officers and professional bodies in the development of the Strategy. Whilst local play strategies will be led by Children's Trusts, this will need to involve close working with the wider Local Strategic Partnership and be effectively joined up with District Councils in two tier authorities.

The Play Strategy also highlights a new indicator for the National Indicator Set (NI199) which will come into effect from April 2009, subject to final technical consultation. This indicator measures children's satisfaction with local parks and play areas.

Current planning and highways policies set out how children's needs should be considered in the development of open space strategies, residential housing, road safety, street design and traffic management. We are asking you to ensure that the spatial needs and road safety of children playing and travelling to play areas are fully reflected in the decision-making of your departments, and would like to highlight how we can support you in your efforts.

Planning support and guidance

Funding for every top-tier local authority – a new investment package of £235 million underpins the Play Strategy over the period 2008-11. Every top-tier local authority will receive at least £1 million to help build and refurbish public play sites where children need them most, with safe access routes which encourage active and healthy journeys, as part of a strategic approach to improving play offers locally. This should complement, rather than substitute for, the investment that local authorities and private developers make.

Play England, Government's national delivery partner for the investment programme, will be able to advise you on when your authority will be receiving funding and who the project leads are. Regional Play England contacts can be found at www.playengland.org.uk

Practice Guidance under PPG17 and PPS3 – Communities and Local Government and the Department for Children, Schools and Families will work with planning and highways officers, the Royal Town Planning Institute, the Department of Health and other stakeholders to provide web-based guidance in support of the policies in PPG17 and PPS3. The guidance, which will be launched in early 2009, will aim to help local authorities to develop effective local strategies for play space and will bring together various standards and good practice on child-friendly place making.

Professional Training – The Play Strategy also announces a programme of cross-professional training. Play England, SkillsActive and Playwork Partnerships are developing a programme to help a range of local professionals, especially those working outside of children's services, to understand the relevance and importance of children's play and how they can support improved play opportunities and safe, active travel for children.

Free training will be rolled out across every local authority by 2011, and will be developed in close co-operation with the professional bodies and Sector Skills Councils. Our intention is to integrate training with current Continuous Professional Development arrangements. The training will be developed and tested between now and April 2009 in our first 20 Pathfinder authorities, which are listed at www.dcsf. org.uk/play. Play England regional offices can advise on how you can get involved.

Road safety – The Child Road Safety Strategy published by the Department for Transport (2007) looks at measures to improve child road safety. Any measures taken by your local authority to improve road safety have the potential to improve access to play at the same time. For example, educational and training initiatives, such as the Kerbcraft child pedestrian training scheme and Bikeability cycle training, will help to make children and young people safer and improve their confidence in making journeys.

Manual for Streets is DfT guidance for the planning, design, provision and approval of new residential streets and modifications to existing ones. It aims to increase the quality of life through good design, which can also support more outdoor play. Engineering measures that can be used to help make play safer include, where appropriate, 20mph zones, as well as smaller scale measures such as improved crossing facilities and junction improvements. Home Zones in urban areas and Quiet Lanes in rural areas, which encourage mixed use of roads with low traffic volumes, can also help to create an environment that encourages children to play outdoors.

Sustrans' Active Play and Travel: Tackling Obesity (APT TO) programme has provided guidance to all Play Pathfinder and Playbuilder authorities on how to ensure children and young people can enjoy independent and active access to play provision. This short checklist can be downloaded from www.sustrans.org.uk/play. Further guidance examining practical ways of delivering safe routes to play will be published by Sustrans early in 2009.

Many thanks in advance for your support on this important agenda for Government.

Steve Quartermain
Chief Planner
Communities and Local Government

Richard Hatfield
Director General
Safety, Service Delivery and Logistics
Department for Transport

Tom Jeffery
Director General Children and Families
Department for Children, Schools
and Families

Professor David R Harper
Director General
Health Improvement and Protection
Department of Health

Andrew Ramsay
Director General,
Partnerships and Programmes
Department for Culture, Media and Sport